The Power of the
ROYAL SCOTS

A new era dawns on Camden Bank — *London Scottish* climbs the gradient in 1928.

Real Photographs

Frontispiece:
Maturity — *The Hussar* at Berkhamsted in 1946.
British Rail LMR

The Power of the
ROYAL SCOTS

Compiled by David Jenkinson

Oxford Publishing Company

Reprinted 1986
ISBN 0-86093-175-7

Printed in Great Britain by Blackwells Printing Ltd., Oxford

'Re-birth' — *Scots Guardsman* at Rotherham 1978.

David Eatwell

Title page:
Twilight years — *Scottish Borderer* in rebuilt form leaving Carlisle in August 1962.

S. C. Crook

Published by:
Oxford Publishing Company
Link House,
West Street,
Poole,
Dorset.

Introduction

The LMS was not a glamorous railway, it had neither the tradition of the GWR nor the panache of the Gresley-inspired LNER. Neither did it enjoy the continuity of the single-minded pursuit of efficiency of Sir Herbert Walker's much smaller Southern Railway. But it was Britain's largest and most important transport undertaking during the inter-war years and the problems it inherited at the Grouping did not disappear simply because of their apparent intractability.

Nowhere was this more manifest than in its locomotive affairs where it simultaneously displayed both the best and the worst of British practice. Inevitably, there were teething troubles and it is a matter of history that these took time to solve. In fact, it was not really until the appearance of the 'Royal Scot' Class of locomotives that the fledgling LMS possessed something approaching a unifying symbol in its motive power department.

Of course, the ultimate unifying force was the eventual arrival on the scene of Sir William Stanier in 1932 and I have never disguised my admiration of this great man's work. But in praising Stanier it is all too easy to forget that the LMS standardisation/rationalisation policy had already started under his predecessor Sir Henry Fowler and there could be no more symbolic representation of this fact than the 'Royal Scot' 4-6-0s.

In many ways the 'Royal Scots' typified the LMS even more than did Stanier's later designs, for they were the one class which accurately reflected both periods. In original form, their design was so highly typical of the early LMS as to be almost a caricature. Yet, when rebuilt on the Stanier principles, they were to become what is generally regarded as Britain's finest express passenger 4-6-0 – not even yielding to the GWR 'Kings' in the all important matter of generated horsepower.

It was therefore with some pleasure that I received the publisher's invitation to compile this book as a companion to my earlier efforts featuring the 'Duchess' Class 4-6-2s; for it seemed to me that, as with the Stanier 4-6-2s, so too with the 'Royal Scots', the phrase 'Power of ---' amply fitted the role of the engines.

Once again, I am particularly indebted to the photographers whose efforts give the book any artistic merit it may possess and my heartfelt thanks go to them all. As with any work devoted to a class of locomotive where the members can no longer be seen in action, it is inevitable that some of the pictures have a familiar look but, as with the 'Duchesses', I have tried to include as much new material as possible – and I find once again, to my surprise, that there has never, so far, been published a full-length pictorial album devoted to these particular engines – so maybe there is still some ground to be broken.

I have tried to tell a chronological picture story of the 'Royal Scots' from start to finish and, as with the 'Duchess' books, I have also tried to put meat on the carcass by employing extended captions whenever they seemed relevant or appropriate. In this context I have been extremely privileged to have enjoyed the help and wisdom of the late Mr. Roland Bond (BR's last steam Chief Mechanical Engineer), whose earlier work for the LMS in seeing these engines into service in their early days is now part of railway history. During the last year or two of his life I spent many happy hours talking steam engines with him and the bulk of the picture selection in this volume was made with the benefit of his advice and kind counselling. The 'Scots' were clearly his 'babies' and I have pleasure in dedicating this book to his memory.

I have often been asked to state my favourite locomotive design – an impossible task to assay. Some designs appeal to the emotions, some to one's artistic sensibility, some because they seem so obviously fitted for their purpose. I think the 'Scots' come in the last category but I doubt if I could ever get it down to one single design on all counts. If the 'Duchess' 4-6-2s appealed to my heart, then the 'Scots' equally appealed to my head – they were so obviously 'right' for the job – and by golly they did some work in their time. This book tries to show how.

David Jenkinson
Knaresborough
1982

The odd man out – No. 46170 *British Legion* at Watford in 1959.
British Rail LMR

Plates 1 and *2 (left):* The NBL Company split the order for fifty engines between the Queens Park and Hyde Park works (twenty-five each). The Queens Park engines (Nos. 6100-24) had diamond pattern works plates on the side of the smokebox and the Hyde Park engines (Nos. 6125-49) had circular plates. The LMS had decided to name the new engines but they were built so expeditiously that when the first examples emerged, names had not yet been decided.

Author's Collection

Plate 3 (below): The 'Scots' were designed to take over the workings previously performed by ex-LNWR types, including the 'Claughton' 4-6-0s. Twenty of these had already been rebuilt with larger boilers to try and enhance their performance and some had additionally been fitted with Caprotti valve gear. The new order is symbolised at Crewe c1929 with Caprotti 'Claughton' No. 5946 *Duke of Connaught*, alongside 'Royal Scot' No. 6115 *Scots Guardsman*.

Gowan Collection
National Railway Museum

Five hundred tons at 55 mph average speeds was the basic yardstick for the 'Royal Scot' design. By 1926 the LMS was beginning to realise that its immediate post-grouping assumption that one could run the new company as a sort of 'Greater Midland Railway' was beginning to have its limitations. The West Coast Main Line simply did not lend itself to the MR 'little and often' practice of lightly loaded trains and double heading was rife, since no suitable single unit of locomotive power was available.

The admirable Midland compound 4-4-0 design had been multiplied in profusion but was too small; Sir Henry Fowler (the LMS Chief Mechanical Engineer) had ideas for a new 4-6-2 which had promise; but the LMS management (unknown to the Chief Mechanical Engineer) had arranged to borrow the GWR *Launceston Castle* 4-6-0 for trials. Confusion and doubt reigned supreme. The 'Castle', as might be expected, showed a clean pair of heels to all the LMS types, so Fowler was told to build a similar 4-6-0 type and abandon his 4-6-2 project. The trouble was that the company shops could not possibly deliver the goods in time for the proposed new summer services in 1927 so the LMS was in trouble. The GWR (naturally) would not lend the 'Castle' drawings so the LMS turned to R. E. L. Maunsell of the Southern Railway whose new 'Lord Nelson' 4-6-0 seemed to be about right. The SR lent drawings of the 'Nelson' and the North British Locomotive Company were asked to produce fifty locomotives in double quick time, loosely based on the 'Nelson' but designed essentially in the Derby drawing office. Fortunately (for the Nelson was by no means perfect at that time) Derby persuaded NBL to go for three cylinders and use valve events based on the highly successful Horwich 2-6-0s and the 'Royal Scots' were born. Although bearing a superficial resemblance to 'Lord Nelson' there was a good deal of Horwich thinking in the design — it was just as well.

Plates 4 to *8:* The original fifty engines were so successful that by 1930, the LMS felt that more could be usefully employed. This time the company could tackle the problem in house as it were, and Derby works was given the order for twenty additional engines embodying detailed improvements based on experience with the NBL series. No. 6155 (later *The Lancer*) of the Derby series (Nos. 6150-69) is seen here in various stages of construction.

         National Railway Museum

Plate 9

PARALLEL BOILER STYLE – PHASE I

By comparison with all earlier LMS locomotive designs the 'Royal Scots' were big machines, the most striking feature being the parallel boiler set with its centre line some 9 ft. 3½ in. above rail level. This left but little room for a chimney on top of the 6 ft. 3 in. diameter smokebox and no attempt was made to improve its relative proportions by surrounding it with a larger casing than the blast orifice demanded. Consequently, it looked rather puny. Moreover, the engines were attached to rather small LMS standard tenders of obvious Midland inspiration. Nevertheless, the engine was suitably impressive and the decision to name some of the engines after famous military regiments and (initially) to name the balance after celebrated earlier steam engines was very popular. The LMS had initially eschewed naming its engines but the revival of a formerly strong LNWR tradition was a welcome step in publicity terms. The term 'Royal Scot' was itself derived from the name given by the LMS to its 10.00 a.m. Anglo-Scottish train. During the first few years, there was a surprising consistency of appearance between members of the class but there were subtle differences between individual examples and the next few pages attempt to illustrate some of them.

Plate 10

Plate 11

◄ *Plates 9* and *10 (left):* The most obvious initial difference between the NBL locomotives such as No. 6121 *H.L.I. (upper)* and the Derby examples like No. 6161 *The King's Own (lower)* was the insignia applied with the famous crimson lake livery. The NBL locomotives received the cabside crests and large tender numbers of the 1923-7 period while the Derby engines came into traffic from new with the post-1927 style of company markings. These two pictures are of engines in photographic grey which helps to clarify the lining style. Detail differences on the Derby batch were the coal rails fitted to the tenders, the additional feed pipe to the snifter valve (on the footplate top, just ahead of the main steam pipe) and the slightly different shape of motion bracket support just below the footplate to the rear of the valve spindle guide.

British Rail LMR

Plate 12

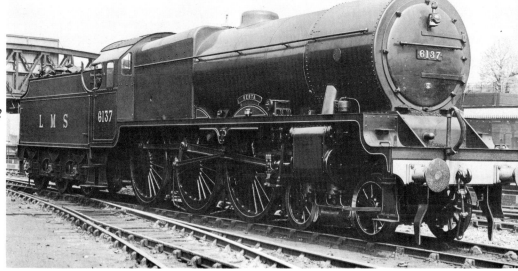

Plates 11 to *13 (right):* In service, the actual lining applied did not always correspond in exact detail with the works grey 'model'. The upper view of No. 6122 *Royal Ulster Rifleman* shows clearly a dark crimson band of paint above the vermilion on the front buffer beam. This was normal with the NBL batch. No. 6137 *Vesta* with the later post-1927 markings shows this dark band even more clearly but in this case the new cabside numbers are in small 10in. hand-painted figures. Finally, No. 6103 *Royal Scots Fusilier* shows a re-lettered NBL locomotive with full vermilion front buffer beam but with 14in. cabside figures of matching height to the tender lettering 'LMS', the cab figures being of LMS standard style with small loops to the '6' rather than the specified Midland style figures seen on No. 6161 *(opposite)*.

Real Photographs and
Author's Collection

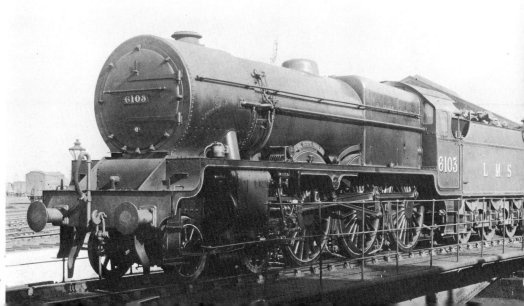

Plate 13

Plate 14

Plates 14 and 15: Further slight livery variations are evident on these two views. No. 6119 *Lancashire Fusilier* on the 'Midday Scot' at Carlisle on 20th April 1929 shows a re-lettered NBL locomotive with 14 in. standard figures combined with dark crimson band on the upper front buffer beam while No. 6116 *Irish Guardsman* is another NBL example, still with two-colour front buffer beam but this time bearing Midland style figures.

Cowan Collection and *British Rail LMR*

Plate 15

Plate 16

Plate 17

Plates 16 and *17 (above):* These broadside views have been included mainly to show the number and letter spacings with the post-1927 LMS insignia. Note that No. 6123 *Royal Irish Fusilier* has, apparently, had its Queens Park NBL plates removed while No. 6125 *Lancashire Witch* still carries its Hyde Park works plates. Both examples show the hand-painted LMS standard figures — somewhat cruder in shape than the MR style — *see Plate 18*.

British Rail LMR

Plate 18: This view shows Derby built No. 6154 *The Hussar* with MR style numbers, full vermilion buffer beam and coal rails on the tender. That the latter were needed is obvious from the picture. Note that, in general, if MR pattern figures were present, the insignia were likely to be gold transfers with black shading whereas the standard LMS shaped figures were hand painted, probably in pale yellow paint.

Author's Collection

Plate 18

DRIFTING SMOKE AND ALL THAT

In 1931, a serious accident at Leighton Buzzard to a 'Royal Scot' hauled train when crossing at too high speed from fast to slow lines brought into question the issue of whether or not the driver's view of the signal had been obscured by drifting smoke and is often cited as the reason for the fitting of smoke deflector plates to the 'Royal Scots'. In point of fact a more likely reason for the derailment (apart from the too high speed) was the somewhat inadequate control given by the front bogie springs in original form — they were later stiffened with beneficial effect.

In any event, the LMS had been conducting smoke deflection experiments for some time prior to 1931, so the 1931 accident cannot have been the sole cause. Some weird and wonderful experimental creations were produced, as the next few pages bear witness. No records have been traced by the author as to the number of different attempts nor to the relative efficiency of these multifarious devices but fortunately most of them succumbed to historical oblivion! The captions also draw attention to further livery and detail points.

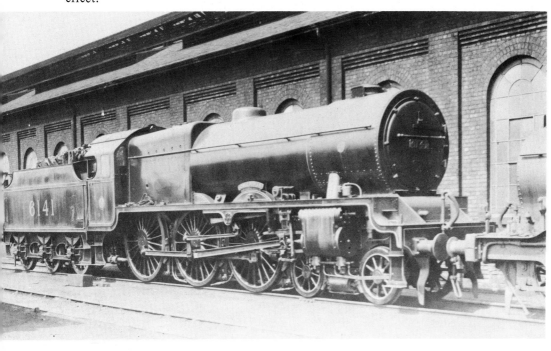

Plates 19 and *20:* The first device, chronologically, seems to have been a so-called 'Gladstone Collar' device fitted behind the chimney of at least two examples, No. 6141 *Caledonian (left)* and No. 6100 *Royal Scot (below).* At least this device was (visually) fairly innocuous. Judging from the liveries carried on the two examples, the date is about the time of the insignia change (c 1928-9). Note the small cabside figures on No. 6100 and the full vermilion front buffer beam on No. 6141.
Author's Collection

Plate 21: The first chimney collar may have been unobtrusive but the later version fitted to No. 6100 was anything but — about 5 ft. long and hardly beautifying. The engine has now acquired Midland pattern 14 in. cabside numerals (c 1930).

Author's Collection

Plate 22: A variant of the chimney collar was fitted to No. 6125 *Lancashire Witch* also c 1930. Note that this engine has also by now received Midland style cab figures (cf *Plate 17*). Clearly, the hand-painted figures were a temporary expedient and probably confined to the 1928 re-paints.

Real Photographs

Plate 23: No. 6151 *Royal Horse Guardsman* saw the collar theme pursued even further, accompanied by modifications to the smokebox top and flared out side-shields. One doubts if the driver could see ahead even *without* smoke from the chimney! Note the coal rails on the tender and the two-colour front buffer beam, the latter a little unusual for a Derby built engine at this time.

Real Photographs

Plates 24 and 25: Another 'guinea pig' was No. 6161 *King's Own* (originally *The King's Own* (see Plate 10). Here, the conical smokebox projection allied to a somewhat more integrated smokebox 'hood' device gave a little more evidence that someone at least was thinking of appearance as well. However, all these various ideas came to naught and the final solution adopted *(below)* was that of traditional smokebox side deflector plates, as seen on No. 6131 *Planet* at Euston on 16th August 1932.

Author's Collection and *Patterson-Rutherford Collection, National Railway Museum*

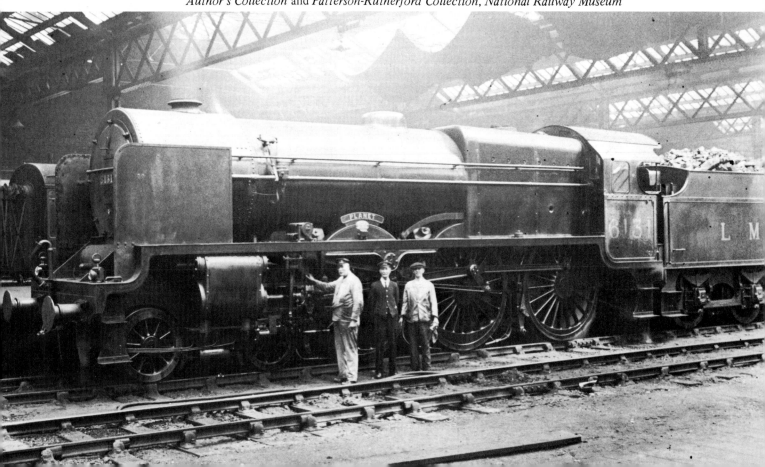

The decision to fit the engines with conventional smoke deflector plates was carried out from 1932 onwards and this inaugurated a period of some four or five years during which the original 'Royal Scots' underwent a considerable series of visual changes. These fell into three principal categories, namely the nature of the smoke deflector plates themselves, further changes in livery styles and the replacement of the original tenders. By the outbreak of war, the various physical alterations had mostly taken place but livery variations continued well into the post-war BR period. The next few pages attempt to unravel the story in approximate chronological order, mention being made of other detail changes where apparent from the pictures.

One general point which is probably worth noting is that with the addition of smoke deflector plates and, later, the 4,000 gallon Stanier pattern tenders, the engines seemed to present an even more massive and 'chunky' appearance — almost as if the boilers had gained a few inches in diameter as well. It was an optical illusion but none the less obvious.

Plates 26 and *27:* The first 'standard' smoke deflector was a straight flat plate seen here on No. 6166 *London Rifle Brigade* and No. 6112 *Sherwood Forester* c 1933. Note that No. 6112 has now acquired coal rails on the tender, as did eventually all the NBL series. This, together with the smoke deflectors obscuring the works plates, made it rather more difficult to identify the NBL locomotives from the Derby built ones but the motion bracket behind the valve spindle guide was still a visual point of difference.

British Rail LMR

Plate 28 (above): The next phase was the change to angled-top deflector plates with the grab handles incorporated on the bottom extension of the plates rather than on the footplate top. This went along with the removal of the bogie brakes and by c1935 most of the engines were in the condition represented by Carlisle based No. 6113 Cameronian.

Author's Collection

Plates 29 and 30: The building of the series of Stanier Class 5XP 4-6-0s in 1935-6 along with the new 4,000 gallon, 9 ton tenders was made the opportunity to effect a major series of tender exchanges, the 'Scots' receiving the new Stanier tenders and handing their smaller ones over to the new 5XPs. These changes took place at yet another change of deflector type to a style with curved-in tops. No. 6119 *Lancashire Fusilier* has the old style *(left)* and No. 6160 *Queen Victoria's Rifleman* the new type *(below)*.

Photomatic and *British Rail LMR*

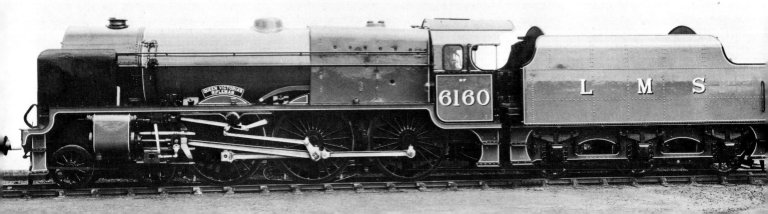

Plates 31 to *34:*   The fitting of Stanier tenders all but coincided with a rapid series of livery and detail changes between 1936 and 1938, but not all engines were modified in the same way at the same time. The main detail changes were the fitting of cabside windshields behind the side windows (and the consequent move of the power class markings below the window), the removal (later) of the crosshead vacuum pump on the left-hand side and the addition of a second rainstrip above the cab windows. The insignia changes went from gold shaded black with MR figures (No. 6129, *above* and No. 6160, *opposite*) via the short-lived gold/red sans serif 1936 style (No. 6145, *above* and No. 6119, *opposite*) and back to the MR style but this time in chrome yellow shaded vermilion (No. 6131, *above*). Note that No. 6131 still retains angled top deflectors even after 1937. The final LMS style is represented by No. 6134 in the glossy black 1946 passenger livery.

All: British Rail LMR

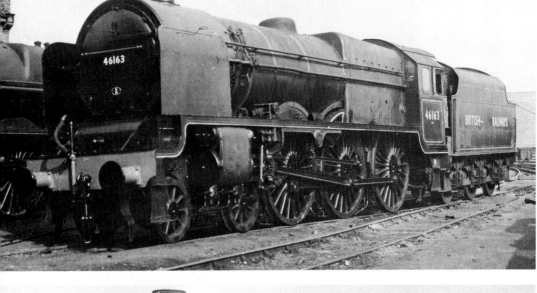

Plate 35

Plates 35 to *37:* The final phase of the parallel boiler 'Scots' moves into the BR period. By now, lifting holes had been added to the front upper frames of some of the engines such as No. 46163 *Civil Service Rifleman* at Crewe in 1949, carrying early BR livery of LNWR style lined black *(above left)*. Another example in LNWR lined black was No. 46156 *The South Wales Borderer* which, when photographed in 1950 *(below left)*, had received shortened front frames above the footplate in the manner of the rebuilt engines. Paradoxically, No. 46151 *The Royal Horse Guardsman*, which remained un-rebuilt for long enough to receive the standard BR green livery *(below)*, received neither front frame lifting holes nor reduced length frames.

T. J. Edgington and *British Rail LMR*

Plate 36

Plate 37

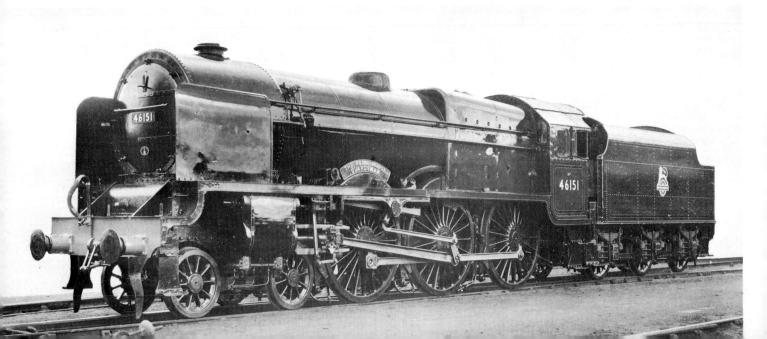

PARALLEL BOILER 'SCOTS' IN DETAIL

Modellers of 'Royal Scots' have a real problem if they are to get things right for different periods of their history. The previous pages have tried to cover some of the more obvious external changes, the next few pages concentrate on close-up details.

Plate 38 (right): Valve gear and footplate detail on Derby built No. 6160 c 1936.

British Rail LMR

Plate 39 (below): The basic 'engine' part of NBL built No. 6107 c 1928.

British Rail LMR

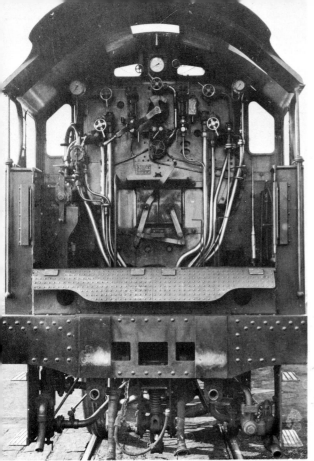

Plate 40   Plate 41   Plate 42

Plates 40 to *42 (opposite):* Footplate and smokebox views c1930 (locomotive unidentified) and low level view emphasising cylinders, bogie brakes, etc., c1932 (locomotive unidentified). Note the very early additions of two extra smokebox door fixing lugs at the base of the smokebox – cf *Plate 39*.

British Rail LMR

Plates 43 and *44 (right):* These cab-end views represent the locomotives at different periods in time. No. 6127 *Novelty* c1934 *(top right)* clearly shows the narrower width of the original tender compared with that of the cab, while No. 46137 c1954 *(below right)* clearly indicates the squat chimney and the slope of the firebox top towards the cab, together with the greater width of the Stanier pattern tender relative to the engine.

Author's Collection and *Alex McNair*

Plate 45 (below): Smokebox view of No. 6116 *Irish Guardsman* fitted with smoke deflectors. Interestingly, the deflectors are of the final type but the engine still has the earlier style shed plate which dates the view as 1935.

British Rail LMR

'ROYAL SCOT' (?) GOES TO AMERICA

In 1933 the LMS sent a locomotive called *Royal Scot* to the Century of Progress exhibition in the USA along with a train of coaches. What is certain is that it was not the original No. 6100, although the official engine history cards do not record any change of identity.

William Stanier was by now CME and it may be supposed that he might have preferred to send one of his new 4-6-2s but they were not ready in time. However, the engine which did go was a very 'Stanierised Scot', if one may thus coin a phrase. It had a full set of Stanier pattern wheels, the Stanier type bogie and many other changes. It also had laminated springs on all three coupled axles. It is certain that the unit which went 'stateside' was a much modified and improved version of one of the Derby built series and the only viable candidate is No. 6152.

Plates 46 and *47 (left):* Proof of the change of identity is given in these two pictures. The 'new' No. 6100 is seen *(above)* at Crewe being prepared for the journey, the motion bracket behind the valve spindle clearly revealing its Derby origins. Evidence of No. 6152 being the original No. 6100 is given below (c1936) with *The King's Dragoon Guardsman* displaying NBL pattern motion bracket – Q.E.D!
British Rail LMR and
Real Photographs

Plates 48 and *49 (opposite):* The ▷ finish given to No. 6100 for its American tour was superb *(above).* Even in this black and white picture it looks impressive. After official photography, the locomotive chassis was separated from the boiler for loading on board ship *(below).*

British Rail LMR

Giants of Speed and Power at A Century of Progress.

Plate 50: Official souvenir post-card of the Century of Progress exhibition. The description of the LMS train as the famous Anglo-Scottish flyer is a bit of a nonsense when the types of carriage are noted. It would have been far more accurate to have described it in similar fashion to the Burlington Train.

Gavin Wilson Collection

The Royal Scot
Famous London-Glasgow-Edinburgh flyer of the London, Midland & Scottish Ry.
1st class corridor brake coach
1st class sleeper coach
3rd class sleeper coach
Lounge car and brake
1st class corridor vestibule coach
Electric kitchen car
3rd class vestibule coach
3rd class corridor brake coach

The Burlington Train
A composite train made up of equipment from regular Burlington trains.
U. S. Railway Post Office car
Reclining chair car (Aristocrat)
Dining car (Black Hawk)
Salon-bed room Pullman (Black Hawk)
14 Section Pullman (Aristocrat)
Lounge car (Ak-Sar-Ben)

The Pride of the Prairies
Engine 35 . . . vintage of 1882. Behind it is a reproduction of the first railway car in which U. S. Mail was assorted in transit, (1862) and thus the actual starting point of today's extensive Railway Post Office service.

Plate 51 (left): The engine fitted with cowcatchers and guarded by 'Mounties' at Montreal, prior to its trip across the Canadian Rockies.

Gavin Wilson Collection

Plate 52 (below): On exhibition at Montreal — head-lamp and bell in position but, as yet, no cowcatcher. The high finish was the subject of much admiration by visitors.

Gavin Wilson Collection

Plate 53 (above): That the 'Scots' were quite sizeable engines is apparent in this picture where it is not entirely dwarfed by Pennsylvania RR 4-6-2 No. 5436, although obviously smaller.

Gavin Wilson Collection

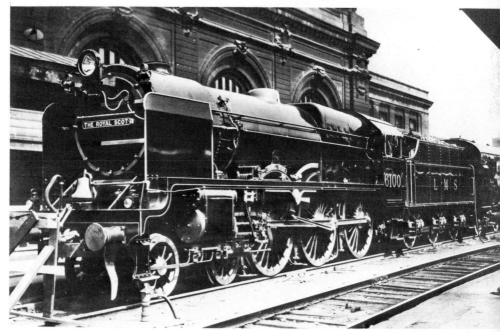

Plates 54 and *55 (right):* Two views on the New York Central system again emphasise the impressive finish and attention to detail of No. 6100 on tour. The lower one gives a good idea of the new tender built for the trip. This was one of three similar tenders, the other two going behind the pioneer Stanier 4-6-2s before the standard Stanier type was evolved.

Gavin Wilson Collection

Plates 56 and *57:* On return to Britain, the locomotive and train were displayed to the public before being returned to traffic. The set is seen *(above)* at Llandudno, a photograph clearly taken after the tour since the engine is fitted with the larger commemorative nameplates seen in close-up *(left).*

British Rail LMR

ROYAL SCOT

THIS LOCOMOTIVE WITH THE ROYAL SCOT TRAIN WAS EXHIBITED AT THE CENTURY OF PROGRESS EXPOSITION, CHICAGO, 1933, AND MADE A TOUR OF THE DOMINION OF CANADA AND THE UNITED STATES OF AMERICA. THE ENGINE AND TRAIN COVERED 11,194 MILES OVER THE RAILROADS OF THE NORTH AMERICAN CONTINENT AND WAS INSPECTED BY 3,021,601 PEOPLE.
W. GILBERTSON. — DRIVER.   T. BLACKETT. — FIREMAN
J. JACKSON. — FIREMAN.   W. C. WOODS. — FITTER.

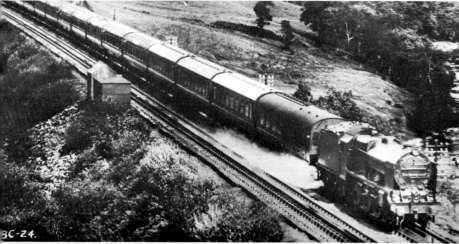

Plate 58: The LMS milked the publicity value of the 'Royal Scot' tour as much as possible, even to the point of doctoring a photograph to form an official souvenir postcard. The train is indeed the real 15-coach 'Royal Scot' on Dillicar Troughs but the engine is not No. 6100. The tender is, clearly, to the normal Fowler pattern and the headlamp, bell and front name have been added by the artist. Goodness knows which engine it really was!

LMS official postcard from
Author's Collection

Plate 59: On return from America the new No. 6100 retained its identity but not the special tender. During 1934-6 it reverted to the Fowler type and then, in due course, received a standard Stanier replacement. It is seen here in early BR days as No. 46100 at Crewe, still carrying the bell but the smokebox now flanked with curved top smoke deflectors.

Author's Collection

WILLIAM STANIER TAKES A HAND

When William Stanier was appointed CME in 1932, the 'Royal Scots' were bearing the brunt of the heavy LMS workings and they continued to play this type of part to the very end, because even when augmented by the later 4-6-2s there were always more 'Scots' available than Pacifics. During the 1930s, Stanier applied many of his own ideas retrospectively to the 'Royal Scots', in order to improve the maintenance and reliability costs, thus ensuring that the engines remained in the top flight as performers.

This they did to a remarkable degree but one senses that Stanier would have preferred to have had a go at a new design, given the chance, embodying more of his own principles than could be applied to the older 'Royal Scot' design. Full rebuilding during the 1940s and 1950s turned out to be the eventual answer but before this event, one interesting locomotive did emerge which showed what a 'Stanier Scot' might look like. It was No. 6170 *British Legion* and emerged as the aftermath of a not very successful experimental high pressure compound 4-6-0 No. 6399 *Fury*.

Plates 60 and *61: Fury* was designed under the supervision of Sir Henry Fowler in collaboration with the Superheater Co. Ltd. and was built in 1929. It was designated, for some reason, as 'Royal Scot' class (*see drawing below*) but was essentially a new concept although embodying a 'Scot' type chassis. The diagram below shows the complex multiple boiler arrangement although the footplate layout (*right*) was fairly conventional.

British Rail LMR and *National Railway Museum*

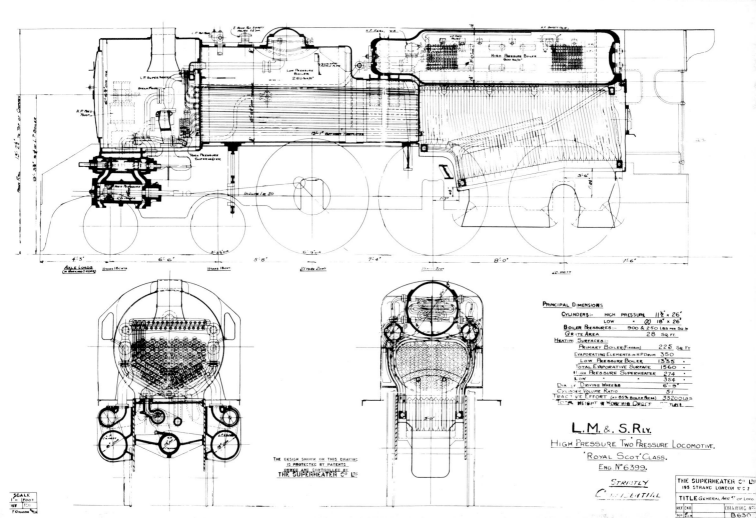

PRINCIPAL DIMENSIONS

CYLINDERS:- HIGH PRESSURE	11½" x 26"	
LOW " (2)	18" x 26"	
BOILER PRESSURES:-	900 & 250 LBS PER SQ IN	
GRATE AREA	28 SQ FT	
HEATING SURFACES:-		
PRIMARY BOILER (FIREBOX)	225 SQ FT	
EVAPORATING ELEMENTS IN H.P DRUM	350 "	
LOW PRESSURE BOILER	1355 "	
TOTAL EVAPORATIVE SURFACE	1560 "	
HIGH PRESSURE SUPERHEATER	274 "	
LOW "	354 "	
DIA. OF DRIVING WHEELS	6'-9"	
CYLINDER VOLUME RATIO	51	
TRACTIVE EFFORT (AT 85% BOILER AREA)	33200 LBS	
TOTAL HEIGHT IN WORKING ORDER		

L. M. & . S. R ly.

HIGH PRESSURE TWO PRESSURE LOCOMOTIVE.
'ROYAL SCOT' CLASS.
ENG N° 6399.

STRICTLY CONFIDENTIAL

THE SUPERHEATER C° LTD
195 STRAND LONDON W.C.2

TITLE GENERAL ARR'T OF LOCO

DRAWING N°
B639

THE DESIGN SHOWN ON THIS DRAWING
IS PROTECTED BY PATENTS
OWNED AND CONTROLLED BY
THE SUPERHEATER C° LTD

Plates 62 to *64:* No. 6399 *(opposite)* was a well proportioned machine, bearing in mind the difficulty of fitting everything within the constricted British loading gauge but on an early trial at Carstairs the experimental boiler 'blew up' with fatal results to the fireman. Experimentation all but stopped and for some years the engine stood somewhat forlorn at Derby *(right)*. Recent investigation of records at the National Railway Museum shows that *Fury* was operated again but with inconclusive results, so the project was abandoned.

British Rail LMR and *Author's Collection*

◁ *Plate 62*

◁ *Plate 63*

Plates 65 and *66:* In 1935, having by then completed the first phase of his standardisation programme, Stanier, prompted heavily by his chief draughtsman, Tom Coleman, took the frames of *Fury* and designed a new taper boiler to fit them. The end result was a typical Stanier engine *(below,* awaiting naming), very similar in appearance to his Class 5 and 5XP 4-6-0s but altogether more powerful in looks and with 'Scot' sized cylinders. It was eventually given highly distinctive nameplates *British Legion (right)*, and became for all practical purposes the 71st member of the 'Royal Scot' Class.

National Railway Museum and
Author's Collection

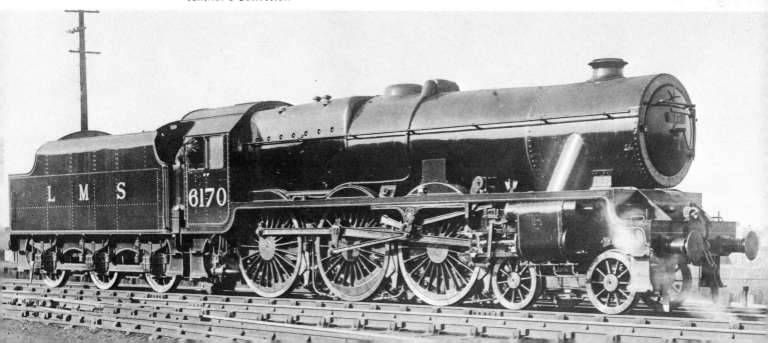

Plates 67 and *68:* It is the author's considered opinion that of all the fine looking engines which emerged during the Stanier regime, *British Legion* in original form was the visual masterpiece. The slightly larger taper boiler than that of the 5XPs gave it an altogether more powerful appearance; while the aggressive thrust forward suggested by the raked back steampipes and slightly elongated smokebox was just right. The classic three-quarter view suited No. 6170 very well whether posed for inspection *(above)* or on its regular working, 'The Mancunian' *(left).*

British Rail LMR and
National Railway Museum

Plates 69 and *70:* Handsome is as handsome does, however, and No. 6170's draughting was not quite correct at first. Tests, including indicating the engine *(left),* suggested several changes, one of which resulted in an alteration to the front steampipes *(below).* The problems were cured but I fancy the appearance suffered a little. Moreover, the later pattern of red-shaded yellow insignia applied in 1937-8 did not sit as well on the engine as did the earlier gold/black *(Plate 67 above).*

Eric Mason Collection – National Railway Museum and *British Rail LMR*

Plates 71 to 73: From any angle, No. 6170 was a good looker as is evidenced by the close-up view from the rear *(above)*, taken after the steampipe change but before the removal of crosshead vacuum pump. The next change was the fitting of a double chimney *(right)*. The engine is seen leaving Carlisle in 1948. Finally, in BR days, *British Legion* received 'Royal Scot' pattern smoke deflector shields *(below)*, becoming visually very similar to the other rebuilds. However, the Stanier cab was still a distinguishing feature and *Legion's* unique boiler was not interchangeable with the standard boiler of the main class.

G. A. Barlow, Gavin Wilson and
Jim Carter

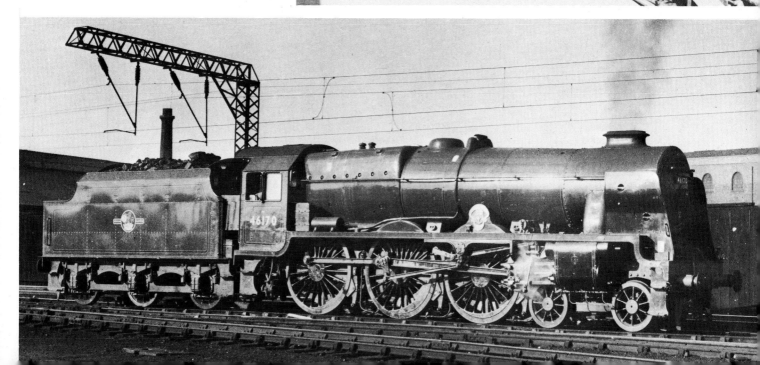

THE 'SCOTS' ARE REBUILT

Plates 74 and 75: The first rebuilds were put in service during the middle of the war and their initial livery was unlined wartime black, as shown by the first rebuild No. 6103 *Royal Scots Fusilier (above)*. At a later stage, the running numbers were raised on the cabside to line up with the letters — giving a better balanced appearance. No. 6104 *Scottish Borderer (below)* is shown with the revised placement. Note also the Stanier pattern coupling rod crankpin on the leading wheels. This engine was rebuilt in March 1946 and the photographic grey livery (with lining) gives some idea how the rebuilds would have looked had the LMS reverted to the traditional crimson livery after the war. This did not happen, so the photograph is somewhat misleading — modelmakers beware!

British Rail LMR

In spite of its early teething troubles, No. 6170 clearly offered an improvement in standard over the existing 'Royal Scots' and when the original parallel boilers fell due for replacement, the LMS resolved to rebuild the whole class on the lines of No. 6170 but using a slightly modified version of the No. 6170 boiler. This new boiler had been applied earlier with great success to two Class 5XP 4-6-0s in 1942. The actual rebuilding of the 'Scots' began in 1943, by which time Stanier had actually left the LMS to take up a different wartime appointment, but the rebuilt (or 'converted') 'Scots' were every inch a Stanier design — some would even say his best. Their appearance was, predictably, very similar to that of No. 6170; but as with the parallel boiler engines, the rebuilds had their detail variations and the next few pages illustrate most of them.

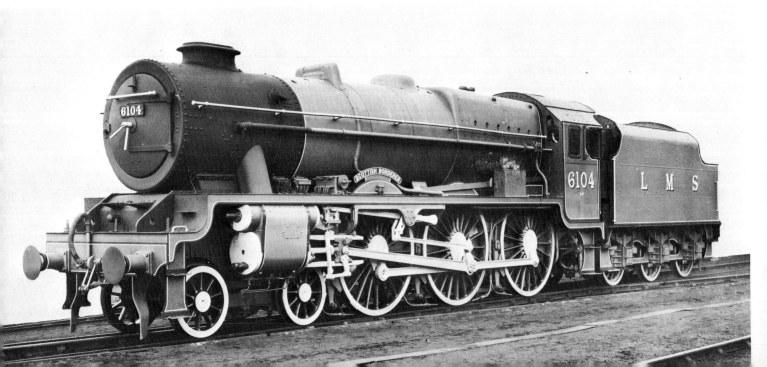

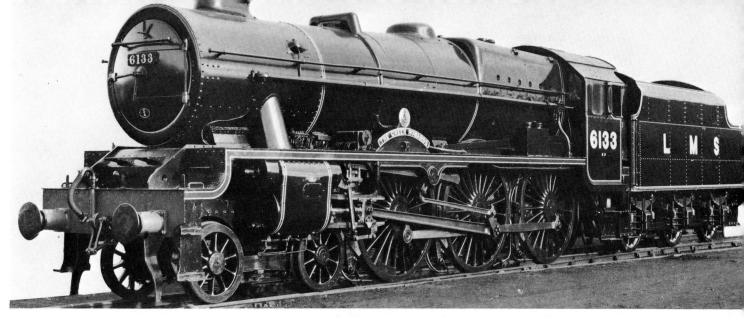

Plate 76 (above): The post-war express livery finally adopted by the LMS was gloss black with maroon and straw lining. No. 6133 *The Green Howards* (also with Stanier pattern leading crankpin) is shown in this style later in 1946 – a very smart turnout when kept clean – but some of us would have preferred to see them red again.

British Rail LMR

Plates 77 and *78:* After nationalisation, experimental colours were tried out by British Railways and the 'Royal Scots' came in for their share. No. 46139 *The Welch Regiment* was painted LNER green *(above)* and No. 46121 *Highland Light Infantry* (formerly *H.L.I.*) in black, both styles with full LNWR lining. Note that the two engines, like many of the earlier rebuilds, retained their Fowler pattern leading crankpins.

British Rail LMR

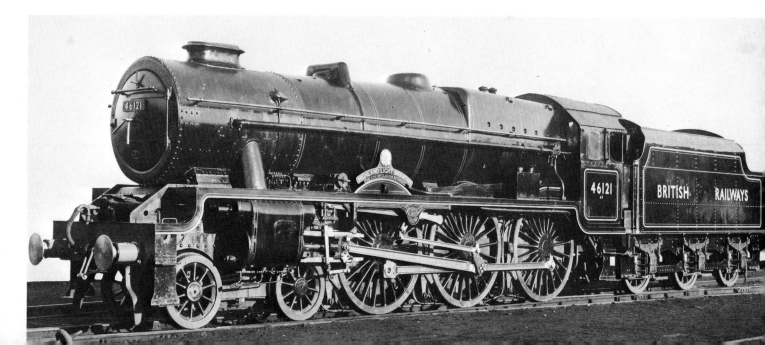

Plates 79 and *80:* The rebuilds were very handsome engines and to all intents and purposes, new machines. Boiler and cylinders were new, as were some of the frames and only the older Fowler cab design revealed that they were not pure Stanier engines. The internally streamlined steam passages and double chimney meant that their blast was less fierce and once again smoke drifting became a problem. Late in 1947, the LMS fitted No. 6115 *Scots Guardsman* with smoke deflectors *(above)* and this became the pattern for the class in BR days. However, 41 out of the 42 converted examples in the LMS period entered BR service without smoke deflectors and it was some time before all were fitted. Opinions differed as to the visual effect of smoke deflectors and for a year or two comparisons could be made such as at Carlisle in 1948 with No. 46115 *Scots Guardsman* alongside No. 46105 *Cameron Highlander (below)*.

British Rail LMR and *Gavin Wilson*

Plates 81 and *82:* It was not until about 1950 that BR decided to fit deflector shields of the LMS pattern to the 'Scots' but there was one exception later, No. 46106 *Gordon Highlander*, which received and retained BR type shields from the mid-1950s *(right upper)*. By all accounts, these were rather more efficient but were not repeated. All the other examples eventually conformed to the *Scots Guardsman* pattern such as No. 46164 *The Artist's Rifleman (right lower)*.

Photomatic

Plate 83: By the 1950s the standard livery for the class was BR green (essentially the old GWR shade) and, interestingly, No.46100 *Royal Scot (below)* was not itself rebuilt until both the green livery and smoke deflectors had been standardised. This engine is now preserved at Bressingham (Norfolk) but in a spurious version of the pre-war LMS crimson lake.

British Rail LMS

Plates 86 to *88 (opposite):* ▷ These views feature, principally, the motion, cylinder and wheel details of *(from top to bottom)* No. 6160 *Queen Victoria's Rifleman,* No. 46148 *The Manchester Regiment* and No. 46170 *British Legion.* Note that No. 6160 is in full back gear, also the BR power classification of 7P prominent on No. 46148 (the LMS classification was 6P) and the non-standard reversing lever on No. 46170.

Photomatic, R. C. Riley and *J. R. Carter*

REBUILT 'SCOTS' IN CLOSE-UP

The reader should, by now, have realised that the 'Royal Scots' were anything but simple locomotives when it came to the question of detail differences. Although these ephemeral variations mattered but little to the operation of the engines in traffic, they are much beloved of enthusiasts and a source of considerable frustration to dedicated modellers. Therefore, as with the case of the parallel boilered engines, an attempt is made on the next few pages to resolve some of the problems in the context of rebuilds.

Plates 84 and *85 (left):* Low level and high level views of No. 46139 *The Welch Regiment* and No. 46155 *The Lancer* respectively.

British Rail LMR and *Norman Kneale*

Plates 89 and *90:* These two pictures feature front end views from opposite sides of, respectively, No. 46169 *The Boy Scout* and No. 46150 *The Life Guardsman.*

British Rail LMR

Plate 91

Plate 92

Plates 91 to *93:* After fitting with smoke deflectors it was not always easy to see the steampipe and smokebox saddle details. These three views of No. 46105 *Cameron Highlander* at Carlisle in 1948, prior to fitting with smoke deflectors, rectify the omission.

Gavin Wilson

Plates 94 and *95:*   These two views of No. 46140 *The King's Royal Rifle Corps* and No. 46130 *The West Yorkshire Regiment* are not only excellent detail shots of the converted 'Scots' — but they are superlative examples of locomotive photography by those two masters of the art, Eric Treacy and Jim Carter respectively.

THE STYLES SUMMARISED

Plates 96 to 99

By way of a conclusion to this first section of the book, the four principal guises of the 'Royal Scots' are illustrated here, spanning the whole period of their life. No. 6130 *Liverpool* is seen *(above)* in original condition at Carlisle in April 1929 while *(below)*, No. 6141 *The North Staffordshire Regiment*, now fitted with smoke deflectors and Stanier tender, is seen in the late 1930s at Brinklow. On the opposite page, No. 6150 *The Life Guardsman* as originally rebuilt by the LMS leaves Manchester London Road with the up 'Mancunian' in 1946 while the lower picture shows No. 46126 *Royal Army Service Corps* in final BR configuration climbing Camden Bank some ten years or so later.

Cowan Collection – National Railway Museum, Gordon Coltas, British Rail LMR and R. C. Riley

Plate 98

Plate 99

'SCOTS' IN SCOTLAND

So far, the survey has confined itself to looking at the evolution of the 'Royal Scots' and their changing appearance over a nearly 40 year life span. It is now time to feature them at work — and what better place to start than in Scotland? After all, the locomotive class name was derived in 1927 from that of the principal LMS Anglo-Scottish express which they were designed to work. Moreover, the LMS even had a special new blend of Royal Scot whisky made to serve in their dining cars — and the brand name still survives, by courtesy of British Transport Hotels. What more recommendation is needed?

Plate 100: Shortly after No. 6130 posed for the picture in Plate 96 *(previous page)* it left Carlisle on a down express for Scotland in front of a very mixed bag of pre-group carriages. Not exactly the 'Royal Scot' train itself, but highly typical of the LMS in the late 1920s.

Cowan Collection
— National Railway Museum

Plate 101: Another random collection of coaches was marshalled for a Glasgow to Keswick excursion behind No. 6104 *Scottish Borderer* on Sunday 19th August 1933, here seen leaving Annan.

Corbett Collection
— National Railway Museum

Plate 102 (above): No. 46110 *Grenadier Guardsman* still unrebuilt, rumbles into Glasgow Central under the Caledonian gantries in early BR days with a down express of LMS standard stock painted BR red and cream.

Author's Collection

Plate 103 (right): The mid-1950s and before the diesel invasion, yet Polmadie based No. 46102 *Black Watch* at Princes Street, Edinburgh is rostered to nothing more important than a stopping passenger train of LMS non-corridor stock.

Eric Treacy

◁ *Plates 104* and *105 (opposite):* The former Glasgow & South Western main line saw the rebuilds from an early date in connection with the through workings to and from Leeds via the Midland route *(see also Plates 236 to 251).* In these views, two Leeds based engines No. 46117 *Welsh Guardsman* and No. 46145 *The Duke of Wellington's Regt. (West Riding)* are seen at Glasgow St. Enoch and Dumfries (respectively) with Leeds bound trains.

Eric Treacy

Plates 106 and *107 (this page):* Like most larger LMS types, the 'Scots' were West Coast Main Line engines above all and remained on this route well into the diesel period. *(Above)* No. 46107 *Argyll and Sutherland Highlander* heads south from Carstairs on 16th June 1962 while *(below)* No. 46166 *London Rifle Brigade* is seen heading north at Gleneagles on one of the demanding Crewe to Perth turns as late as 21st September 1963. The connecting Crieff train (Class 5 hauled) is in the bay to the right.

Derek Cross

'SCOTS' AT LARGE

The 'Royal Scots' were brought into service rapidly in the autumn of 1927 and immediately set to work on the heaviest of the LMS West Coast trains. They were an instant success and continued to perform these arduous duties with conspicuous distinction for the rest of their careers both before and after rebuilding. Mr. E. S. Cox has estimated that most of them probably achieved between two and three million revenue miles each, getting better as they got older. The railway undoubtedly got value for money and on this and succeeding pages an attempt is made to show the nature of their task, emphasis being given to their main galloping ground, the West Coast Main Line.

Plates 108 and *109:* Within days of their introduction, the 'Scots' were rostered for as many of the principal LMS expresses as there were locomotives available and no trains were more prestigious than the 'Royal Scot' and 'Mid-Day Scot' services. Above, the latter train, still containing a fair number of the celebrated twelve-wheelers built for the '2 p.m.' service in 1908 is seen approaching Crewe in 1928 behind No. 6112 *Sherwood Forester*. The lower view, also at Crewe at about the same time, shows No. 6134 *Atlas* departing with the fourteen-coach 'Royal Scot' train, the leading vehicle being one of the first-class lounge brakes built for this service.

Real Photographs and *Author's Collection*

Plate 110: Camden Bank c 1930 with No. 6116 *Irish Guardsman* in charge of the 1.40 p.m. ex-Euston.

Real Photographs

Plate 111: Euston in 1928 still looked very London and North Western. The train is, once again, the down 'Mid-Day Scot' with a strengthening vehicle behind the locomotive, No. 6111 *Royal Fusilier*.

Author's Collection

Plate 112: The 'Royal Scot' c 1930 was regularly made up to fifteen bogies and is seen here in the London suburbs heading north behind No. 6132 *Phoenix*. The leading coach is an 'all steel' full brake, a type which the LMS liked to marshal behind the engine (when possible) as a sort of accident insurance!

Photomatic

Plate 116

Bushey Troughs

Plates 113 to 118: There was something about water troughs which attracted photographers like flies to a honey pot. Nowhere was this more the case than at Bushey, within very convenient range of Central London by local train. Here are some typical scenes from the 1928 to 1936 period.

Above left, No. 6158 *The Loyal Regiment* takes a last fill as it heads south with a lightweight train, probably from Merseyside or North Wales. The leading coach is one of the lounge brakes demoted from 'Royal Scot' service after the building of new stock in 1929-30. Note the lack of coal rails on the tender of this Derby built engine — somewhat unusual. *Left centre,* shows No. 6112 *Sherwood Forester* with a down Lancashire bound train c1931 while *below left,* a similar train is seen at much the same spot some three or four years later behind No. 6109 *Royal Engineer,* now fitted with smoke deflectors.

Plate 117

On this page, the upper view shows No. 6127 *Novelty* in much the same position as No. 6112 *(opposite centre)* but it is now 1934 and the old LNWR signal has been replaced. Note the wonderful collection of five strengthening pre-group corridor coaches at the head of an otherwise tidy set of LMS standard vehicles. *Right centre,* depicts No. 6168 *The Girl Guide* heading the up 'Mancunian'. The first three vehicles are a strengthening 'Inter-Corridor' set at the front of the main seven coach train. The last picture shows No. 6142 on the up 'Ulster Express' in 1936. The engine is now fitted with a Stanier tender but still carries its original name *Lion.* Note, once again, the lounge brake leading.

Photomatic and *Real Photographs*

Plate 118

Plates 119 and *120:* By the later 1930s, the second NBL batch of 'Scots' had lost their original names and assumed the 'regimental' theme of most other members of the class. On this page, No. 6144 *(above)* formerly *Ostrich* had become *Honourable Artillery Company* when photographed c1937 at Kilburn while *left,* No. 6142 formerly *Lion (see Plate 118)* is now *The York & Lancaster Regiment* as it heads north at Bletchley in 1938.

Eric Treacy and *Gordon Coltas*

Plates 121 and *122:* By 1946, the railways were looking pretty scruffy and even the summer sunshine could not enhance the appearance of a grimy No. 6123 *Royal Irish Fusilier (above)* as it headed for Liverpool with the 3.45 p.m. ex-Euston on 25th July. However, things were not always perfect in the pre-war era. No. 6120 *Royal Inniskilling Fusilier* was not in exactly pristine external condition in June 1939 when leaving Northchurch Tunnel *(right).*

British Rail LMR and
H. C. Casserley

Double Heading

Plates 123 to 125: It was a rare occurrence for 'Royal Scots' to be double-headed but it did happen from time to time — probably as often as not to provide a balancing working for a second locomotive. There seems to be no good reason *(above)* for No. 6137 *Vesta* to be receiving assistance from LMS Compound No. 1118 on the down 'Royal Scot' at Watford c1931. There are, it is true, sixteen coaches on the train but that was not abnormal for a 'Scot' on its own.

British Rail LMR

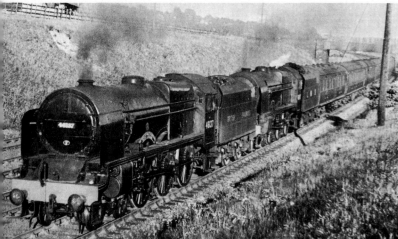

In early BR days, some of the surviving parallel boiler 'Scots' may have been a little war-weary and more in need of double heading. *(Left above)* shows No. 46137 now *The Prince of Wales's Volunteers South Lancashire* and No. 6110 *Grenadier Guardsman* providing almost super-power to a down train at Northchurch in May 1948; while later that year, in September, No. 46106 *Gordon Highlander* receives help from Class 5 4-6-0 No. 45394 at Berkhamsted. Modellers may be interested to note that the 'Scot' is still in LMS crimson lake livery with its BR number.

H. C. Casserley

Plates 126 to *128:* A last look (for the moment) at the parallel boiler 'Scots' in LMS days shows *(above)* No. 6149 *Lady of the Lake* arriving at Crewe under the famous signal gantry with the 2.40p.m. ex-Euston on 11th September 1934. On the right, No. 6117 *Welsh Guardsman* is seen in pre-smoke deflector days at Castlethorpe Troughs c1930 while *(below)* No. 6145 *The Duke of Wellington's Regiment* leaves Rugby with a Liverpool express in June 1939.

Corbett Collection – National Railway Museum,
Author's Collection and *Gordon Coltas*

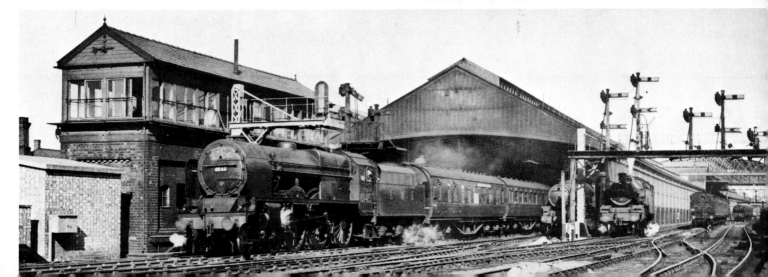

Plates 129 to *131:* Elderly they may have been but many of the surviving parallel boiler 'Scots' in early BR days were still capable of feats of prodigious haulage and were worked turn and turn about with the rebuilds and the Stanier 4-6-2s. *(Above)* No. 46141 *The North Staffordshire Regiment* sets off up Camden Bank in 1948 with little apparent fuss and a nice clean exhaust while opposite *(above)* the last of the parallel boiler engines No. 46137 *The Prince of Wales Volunteers* seems to be having no trouble in taking at least fifteen bogies (including some of the heavy BR Mk. I stock) over the top of Camden Bank in the early 1950s.

Amongst the heavyweight trains at this time was the 'Lakes Express' and No. 46140 *The King's Royal Rifle Corps (opposite below)* is in charge of yet another fifteen coach load seen southbound at Tring in July 1950. Note the shortened front frames on all three engines depicted on these pages.

Eric Treacy and *British Rail LMR*

THE REBUILDS TAKE OVER

The rebuilt 'Scots' with their tapered boilers were visually so well proportioned that they never looked anything like as powerful or massive as the parallel boiler engines — and this contrast was especially noticeable in the early years when the rebuilds ran without smoke deflectors alongside the surviving parallel boiler types. However, as has been mentioned, the rebuilt locomotives were, to all intents and purposes, new engines and they quickly began to show their mettle. There seemed to be nothing they could not tackle and to those modern-day enthusiasts who get ecstatic about a 3,300hp 'Deltic' running at 100mph with ten bogies as though it was remarkable, it is perhaps worth mentioning that the nominally not much more than half as powerful 'Scots' regularly hauled 50% larger trains at 75mph or more and they did it as a result of skilled men working hard and not simply by pressing a switch and pulling a lever!

Plates 132 and *133:* No. 6118 *Royal Welch Fusilier* is seen *(above)* at Crewe waiting for departure and still wearing full LMS livery in September 1948. *(Below)* No. 6118 making light work of at least sixteen bogies as it traverses Castlethorpe Troughs at speed on a different occasion.

D. P. Rowland and *Real Photographs*

Plate 134 (left): A typical early BR scene at Cheddington in July 1950 shows No. 46111 *Royal Fusilier*, still in LMS colours, on a train of mixed LMS and BR liveried vehicles.

British Rail LMR

Plates 135 and *136 (opposite):* Eric Treacy ▷ reckoned that the rebuilt 'Scots' (prior to fitting with smoke deflectors) were his favourite engines in visual terms. He certainly took some evocative pictures of them, like No. 6101 *Royal Scots Grey* c1946 *(above)* and No. 46154 *The Hussar* leaving Euston *(below).*

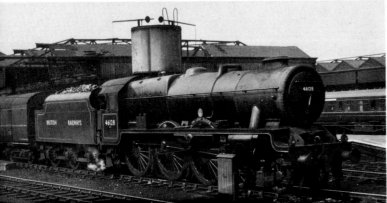

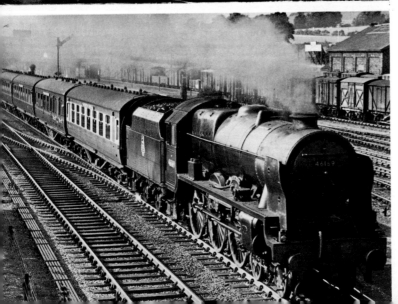

Plates 137 to 141: By the late 1940s and early 1950s many of the wartime arrears of maintenance were beginning to be overcome and standards of cleanliness improved. Not surprisingly, the 'Royal Scots' benefited from these improved conditions and for the next ten years or so were probably at their all-time best. On this page *(top)*, No. 46143 *The South Staffordshire Regiment* sets off from Euston in 1950 with the down 'Mancunian' while No. 46128 *The Lovat Scouts (left centre)* waits at Crewe —both engines in experimental LNWR lined black colours. By 1951, BR green was the standard livery for the 'Scots' and No. 46169 *The Boy Scout*, seen at Tring in July 1951 *(left below)* with an up Manchester express is obviously fairly fresh off works. Opposite are illustrated No. 46153 *The Royal Dragoon* on the down 'Shamrock' leaving Euston in the early 1950s and No. 46136 *The Border Regiment* almost camouflaged by the shadows of the station roof at Carlisle at much the same period.

Eric Treacy, Author's Collection and *British Rail LMR*

Plate 140 ▷

Plate 141 ▷

In due course, the rebuilds just about got everywhere and by way of conclusion to this section, this set of pictures shows some of the many places they visited.

Plates 142 to 144: (Above) No. 46127 *Old Contemptibles* pilots 'Jubilee' No. 45563 *Australia* out of Huddersfield with the 5.00 p.m. Liverpool to Newcastle express in July 1962. Double-heading on this route was not uncommon. *(Left above)* sees No. 46111 *Royal Fusilier* at St. Annes on a Blackpool to Euston express in April 1959 while *(left below)* we get our first view of a 'Royal Scot' on the Midland main line, No. 46133 *The Green Howards* leaving St. Pancras on 6th July 1960. This was, prior to its transfer to Kentish Town shed, one of the celebrated Holbeck 'Scots' – *(see Plates 236 to 251).*

J. R. Carter, Photomatic and *British Rail LMR*

Plates 145 to *147:* On this page *(above)* the odd man out, No. 46170 *British Legion*, passes Springs Branch, Wigan in September 1956 with a Barrow to Euston express, the leading coach indicating that the all-maroon BR carriage livery has just begun to appear. To the right *(above)* No. 46163 *Civil Service Rifleman* is seen at Preston in charge of a London to Perth train a year or two later; while the last picture shows No. 46124 *London Scottish* at Dillicar in the Lune Valley on 2nd August 1962 with an empty stock train; a slight fall from grace but still a heavy load.

Photomatic and *British Rail LMR*

'ROYAL SCOTS' IN COLOUR – I

Colour photography was in its infancy during the pre-war period so I have had to resort to a little subterfuge, via the preserved 'Royal Scots', to adequately illustrate the LMS period.

Plates 148 and *149:* The first picture is taken from a rare pre-war colour transparency and shows No. 6149 *The Middlesex Regiment* ex-shops at Crewe in April 1937 wearing the red shaded yellow insignia of this period. *(Below)* is a view of the preserved No. 6100 *Royal Scot* at Bressingham in May 1973 in pseudo-LMS livery. This engine was never red as a rebuild but the colour chosen is very accurate even if the insignia are somewhat overimaginative in their elaboration!

CCQ Slides and *Gavin Wilson*

Plate 152: Rebuilt No. 46113 *Cameronian* leaves Dumfries with the down 'Thames-Clyde' express in June 1959. The engine would, almost certainly, have worked through from Leeds.

CCQ Slides

Plate 153: By 1964, the survivors were not always very clean. No. 46162 *Queen's Westminster Rifleman* is distinctly scruffy in this view in the Lune Gorge, May 1964, of an Oxley-Carlisle freight.

Gavin Wilson Collection

Plate 154: Freight haulage again in later years, this time No. 46141 *The North Staffordshire Regiment* leaving Oxenholme c 1963, with the banker doing its fair share of the work.

Gavin Wilson Collection

◁ *Plates 150* and *151:* Close-up views of the two preserved 'Scots'; No. 6100 *Royal Scot (left)* at Bressingham in LMS crimson and No. 6115 *Scots Guardsman (right)* at Dinting correctly wearing the 1946 LMS livery. These two colour schemes (along with **BR** green) were the three most common styles of treatment for the class and although No. 6100 is, to the purist, incorrectly liveried, the style applied (insignia excepted) does give an excellent representation of the pre-war LMS treatment.

Gavin Wilson

Plate 155: The real work started at Oxenholme at the foot of the northbound climb to Grayrigg. The gradient on the main line is very clear from the view above, which shows No. 6138 *The London Irish Rifleman* coasting down the bank past the junction with the Windermere line at the head of a twelve coach Manchester express c 1934/5. It is a fair assumption that it had climbed to Shap from Carlisle unassisted with this load.

British Rail LMR

'SCOTS' ON THE LANCASTER AND CARLISLE

Although the 'Royal Scots' were built initially for service on all the principal LMS services on the former LNWR main lines, it was undoubtedly the heavier gradients north of Lancaster and in Scotland which had taxed their predecessors most. Consequently, the hill-climbing ability of the 'Scots' was under close scrutiny from the start. Nowhere was this more crucial than on the route over Grayrigg and Shap from Lancaster to Carlisle. It seems fair to say that the 'Scots' did not let the railway down and the next few pages feature this aspect of their work. By way of a change, this survey is arranged geographically from south to north, rather than chronologically by time period.

Plates 156 and *157 (opposite):* These two almost identical ▷ views of Oxenholme are separated by some thirty years — and a fair amount of tree clearance! *(Above)* No. 6115 *Scots Guardsman* wearing Caledonian route indicators on the smokebox sets off unassisted c 1934 with the twelve coach 'Mid-Day Scot' (GWR through coach leading) without the help of a banker; while *(below)* during the run-down period of the class, rebuilt No. 46160 *Queen Victoria's Rifleman*, shorn of its nameplates, tackles a similar tonnage (albeit one vehicle less) on 31st July 1964 with some rear end help.

Real Photographs and *Derek Cross*

Grayrigg and the Lune Valley

Between the top of Grayrigg Bank and Tebay, the Lune Valley affords a spectacularly beautiful route through the hills prior to the assault on Shap itself and the wide open spaces give a real opportunity to see trains in a country environment.

Plates 158 and *159:* On this page *(top left)* No. 6146 *The Rifle Brigade* is seen descending southbound near Grayrigg c1936 with a Glasgow to Euston train. The engine is sporting the short-lived 1936 sans serif insignia. It is seen passing a northbound train of empty LNER coke wagons, destined, no doubt, for North East England via Tebay and Stainmore. The centre view shows an August 1962 scene with rebuilt No. 46127 *Old Contemptibles* on a parcels working.

Real Photographs and *British Rail LMR*

Plates 160 to *162:* My friend Derek Cross was one of the pioneers in the art of railway landscape photography and like myself, his qualifications include geology. He is, in consequence, very much aware of the relationship between railways and their natural environment and during the latter days of steam brought an almost new dimension to railway pictures. Three typical examples in the Lune Valley, featuring 'Royal Scots', are represented here. *(Below)* No. 46165 *The Ranger (12th London Regt.)* is seen passing Hay Fell (Peat Lane Bridge) in July 1962 with a Liverpool to Glasgow train while *(opposite above)* the same locomotive has steam to spare as it wheels a fourteen coach Glasgow to London relief southbound in July 1963. Finally, backed by the heather-covered hillsides, (now, alas, despoiled by the M6 motorway), No. 46107 *Argyll and Sutherland Highlander* heads towards Tebay with a Manchester to Glasgow express in July 1962.

Derek Cross.

Plate 161

Plate 162

Dillicar Troughs

Plates 163 to *167:* It is a moot point whether more pictures were taken of Dillicar Troughs than of those at Bushey *(Plates 113* to *118)* but there is little doubt which were the more scenically attractive or, perhaps, the more essential, operationally. On this page are seen No. 6137 *Vesta*, northbound in the early days of the 'Royal Scots' (c1930) with a thirteen coach train *(top)*. Next is No. 6153 *The Royal Dragoon* with a lightweight Aberdeen train c1934/5, the second coach being one of the ex-CR· Grampian type twelve wheelers; and finally, a southbound train from Glasgow to Manchester, probably on the same day, is seen behind No. 6127 *Novelty*. On the opposite page, more modern scenes are represented by an unidentified rebuild heading south on 28th June 1961 on a Glasgow to Manchester express *(upper)* and No. 46121 *Highland Light Infantry* nicely managing to completely fill its tank as it reaches the end of the troughs with a Perth to Euston train during the later 1950s.

Author's Collection, Real Photographs, Derek Cross and *Eric Treacy*

Plate 168 (above): Halfway up Shap at Greenholme on 27th June 1963, rebuild No. 46114 *Coldstream Guardsman* is seen climbing well with a nice clean exhaust on a 400 ton train.

Derek Cross

Plate 169 (left): The south-bound climb to Shap from Carlisle could be tough — but not with a rebuild in good order and only nine coaches to pull. No. 46135 *The East Lancashire Regiment* blows off steam near Thrimby woods as it makes light work of the job in the late 1950s.

Eric Treacy

Plates 170 and *171:*   The classic ascent of Shap in steam days — thirteen on, no bankers, no undue fuss, situation normal — was repeated time after time with the 'Royal Scots'. *(Above)* No. 6133 *The Green Howards* c1936/7 (carrying the 1936 insignia) while *(below)* in August 1960, rebuild No. 46106 *Gordon Highlander* (with BR type smoke deflectors) is seen doing much the same sort of job.

Photomatic and *Derek Cross*

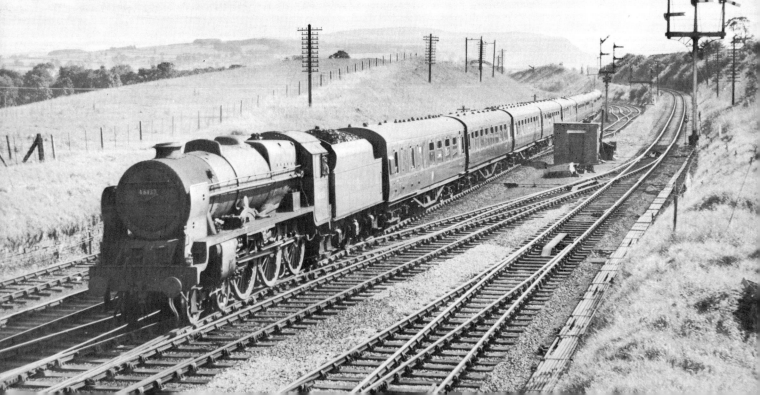

Plates 172 and *173 (opposite):* At Penrith it is downhill one way and very much uphill the other as these pictures make only too clear. *(Above)* No. 46104 *Scottish Borderer* tackles the southbound climb to Shap in the mid-1950s with some 450 tons of Glasgow to Manchester express while *(below)* No. 46133 *The Green Howards* takes life more easily with the northbound Liverpool to Glasgow in July 1963, Keswick branch to the right. This latter picture was almost certainly taken from the signal box visible above the train in the upper picture.

Eric Treacy and Derek Cross

Plates 174 and *175:* The first part of the southbound ascent to Shap started only a few hundred yards south of the platforms at Carlisle. *(Above)* No. 6163 *Civil Service Rifleman* is already on the hill with the southbound 11.53 a.m. (date unknown) while *(below)* rebuild No. 46126 *Royal Army Service Corps* makes a vigorous southbound start in the early 1950s.

Real Photographs and Eric Treacy

'ROYAL SCOTS' IN COLOUR – II

Plate 176 (top): No. 46109 *Royal Engineers*, one of the well-known Leeds based 'Scots', is seen here departing its home city with a Carlisle bound express c1957. This part of the station (the old Midland side) is now nothing more glamorous than a parcels depot.

Jim Carter

Plate 177 (centre): Another Leeds engine No. 46117 *Welsh Guardsman* awaiting to leave St. Pancras with the down 'Robin Hood' towards the twilight of its career.

Colour Rail

Plate 178 (bottom): The sunlight casts an intricate shadow pattern on No. 46116 *Irish Guardsman* at Carlisle in the early 1950s.

Gavin Wilson

'SCOTS' ON SHED

Plates 179 to *181:* The 'Scots' were shedded far and wide but it does not seem inappropriate to start this survey with a series of colour pictures taken at Crewe, where they were all repaired and many were shedded. Driver Jim Carter took the pictures which *(top* to *bottom)* feature No. 46170 *British Legion,* No. 46127 *Old Contemptibles* (the two engines with the highly distinctive non-standard nameplates) and No. 46166 *London Rifle Brigade.* The yellow cabside stripe was applied to engines prohibited from passing 'under the wires' south of Crewe from 1964 onwards.

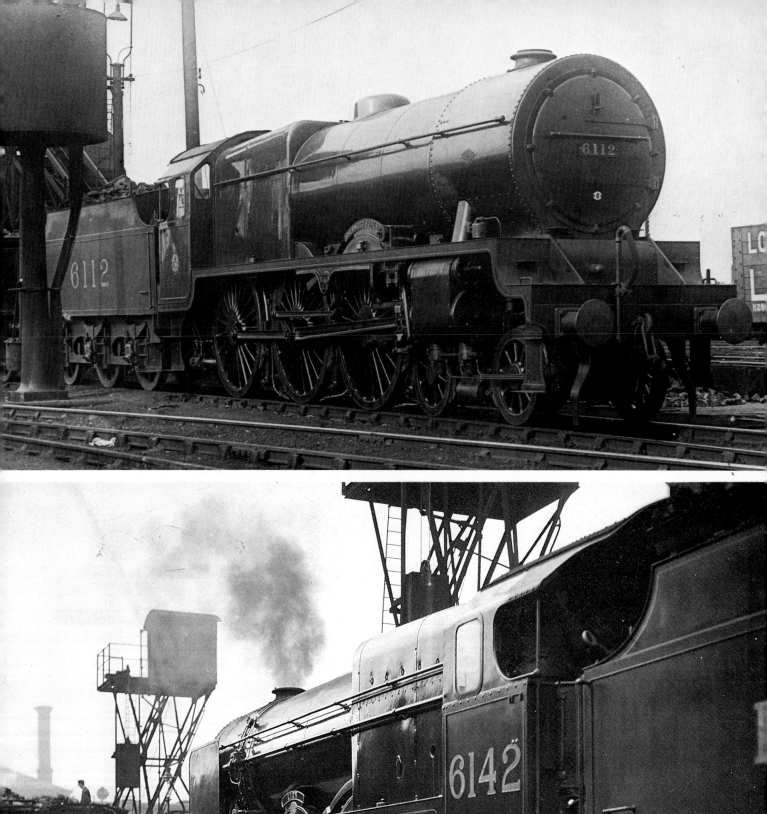

Plates 182 to 187: The 'Royal Scots' were always allocated over a wide geographical area. *(Opposite top)* No. 6112 *Sherwood Forester* is seen at Crewe almost brand new, wearing the No. 8 shed plate of Rugby. *(Below)* A few years later No. 6142 *Lion* was photographed at Camden on 6th May 1933. On this page, No. 6147 *Courier (above)* and No. 6102 *Black Watch (right)* were both photographed at Polmadie in 1932 although *Courier* is wearing the shed plate of Crewe North. *(Below right)* No. 6164, a Crewe North engine, had worked to Perth in August 1939 while finally, No. 46148 *The Manchester Regiment* was allocated to and photographed at Crewe on 30th June 1951 *(below)*.

Real Photographs, H. C. Casserley, Gordon Coltas, Photomatic, Gavin Wilson and *John Edgington*

Plates *188* to *191:* Holyhead was the depot for the North Wales services (including the Irish boat trains) and 'Scots' were seen there most of their life. This page features two of the well-known rebuilds allocated to Holyhead in the immediate post-nationalization period; No. 46127 *Old Contemptibles* and No. 46132 *The King's Regiment Liverpool*. The variations of livery and front numberplate design are interesting, reflecting the slightly experimental nature of the early BR period.

Eric Treacy

Plates 192 to 194: There were always 'Royal Scots' to be seen at Camden, whether based there or working from other depots. These three scenes from the 1950s show *(above)* No. 46161 *King's Own* in July 1950, having worked from Holyhead, No. 46168 *The Girl Guide (right)*, a home engine being readied for the down 'Ulster Express' and *(below)* No. 46167 *The Hertfordshire Regiment* and No. 46148 *The Manchester Regiment* ready and waiting for duty on 21st August 1955.

British Rail LMR and *R. C. Riley*

Plates 195 and *196:* Similar views but at widely separated locations. *(Above)* No. 46140 *The King's Royal Rifle Corps* is being very smartly turned out at Edge Hill while *(left)* No. 46161 *King's Own*, slightly less clean, is seen visiting Bristol c1960.

Eric Treacy and
Author's Collection

Plate 197: No. 46117 *Welsh Guardsman* stands at the head of a row of BR standard types at its home base, Holbeck.

John Whiteley

Plate 198: The now preserved No. 46115 *Scots Guardsman* was quite widely travelled in its later years. At the time of this picture at Willesden, its home base was Manchester, Longsight.

R. C. Riley

Plate 199: This picture of No. 46118 *Royal Welch Fusilier* standing alongside an ex-GWR 2-8-0 at Hereford, affords an interesting visual comparison between the Stanier breed and one of the designs of his mentor at Swindon, G. J. Churchward.

R. C. Riley

Plates 200 to *203:* These evocative scenes were taken by driver Jim Carter from his position of advantage as a footplate cameraman. *(Above)* No. 46144 *Honourable Artillery Company* and No. 46163 *Civil Service Rifleman* complete their preparations at Patricroft for working night trains to North Wales in May 1962; while, *(below)* No. 46165 *The Ranger (12th London Regt.)* was a visitor to Wigan Springs Branch in 1959. Note the slightly non-standard nameplate fitted to this engine. The views opposite show No. 46155 *The Lancer* at Patricroft in 1964 for the Manchester to Llandudno club train and No. 46167 *The Hertfordshire Regiment* also at Patricroft in July 1961 with Class 5 No. 45449.

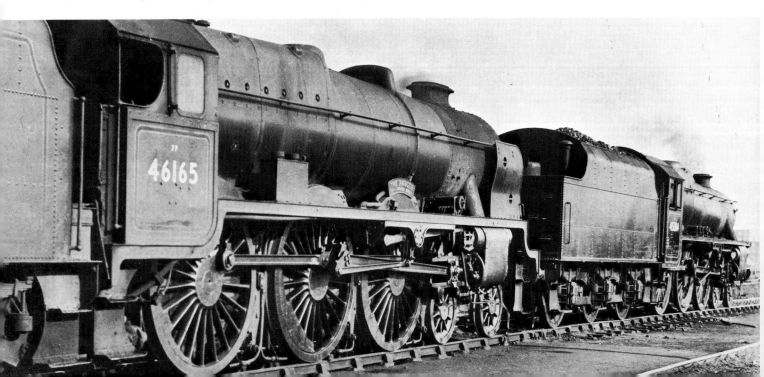

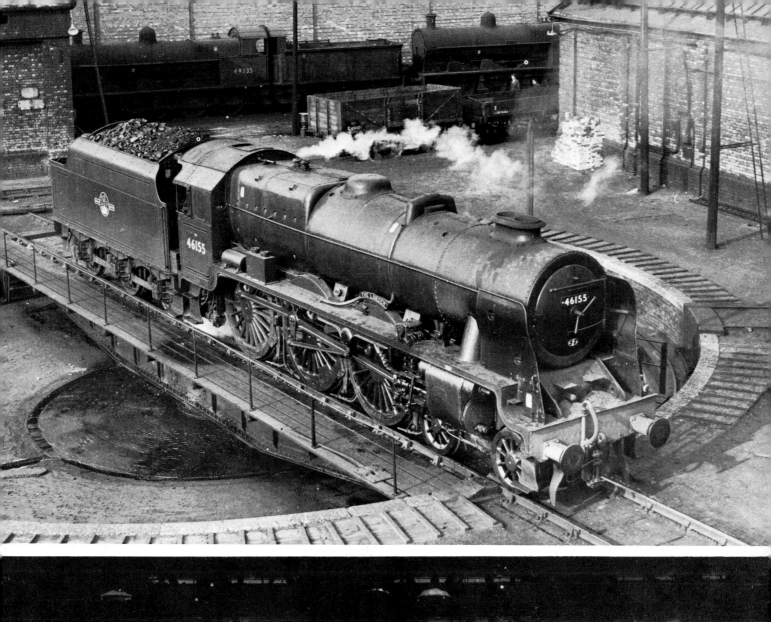

LIVERPOOL AND NORTH WALES

In addition to their strong representation on the West Coast route, the 'Royal Scots' were also very much a part of the Merseyside and North Wales scene. Their workings embraced the direct services to London and Scotland, cross-country expresses to Leeds and Newcastle, boat trains and excursions along the North Wales coast and many more. The next few pages give a visual reminder of some of these workings.

◁ *Plates 204* and *205 (opposite):* It would be unthinkable to prepare a book involving the 'Royal Scots' on Merseyside without including a representative collection of pictures by the late Bishop Eric Treacy who did so much to bring this area of England to the notice of enthusiasts. Two of his classic views are given here, No. 46144 *Honourable Artillery Company* departing from Lime Street station and No. 46124 *London Scottish* in the tunnel on the climb to Edge Hill. They may have been published before – but who cares?

Eric Treacy

Plate 206 (right): The climb to Edge Hill through the cuttings and tunnels could be a bit like Dante's 'Inferno' in steam days but eventually one reached the daylight. No. 46119 *Lancashire Fusilier* bursts into the sunlight at Edge Hill with a Liverpool to Newcastle train in the late 1950s, the first two vehicles being a Gresley articulated twin set looking suspiciously like ex-streamline stock.

Alex McNair

Plate 207 (right): The Liverpool to Newcastle trains alternated between LMS and LNER stock well into BR days. In this view, No. 46142 *The York & Lancaster Regiment* is seen at Earlestown on 21st August 1957 on the LMS set, albeit diluted towards the rear with a few BR Mk. I coaches.

L. Elsey

Plates 208 to *210:* The London bound traffic turned right at Edge Hill and headed south via Wavertree. This was another Eric Treacy area and three prime examples of his work are featured here. *(Above)* No. 6126 *Royal Army Service Corps* turns south at Edge Hill c1937, while opposite *(above)* No. 6144 *Honourable Artillery Company* is seen a little further south vigorously attacking the climb towards Wavertree. Finally *(opposite below)* rebuild No. M6138 *The London Irish Rifleman* tops the bank near Wavertree in 1948 with a massive load of at least thirteen or fourteen bogies.

Eric Treacy

Plates *213* and *214: (Above)* No. 46144 *Honourable Artillery Company* heads the up 'Emerald Isle' express near Saltney Junction on 27th June 1962 while *(below)* No. 46148 *The Manchester Regiment* is seen at its home base, Llandudno Junction, with a stopping passenger train.

Derek Cross and *Norman Kneale*

◁ Plates *211* and *212:* The Chester and Holyhead was another celebrated section of the old LNWR. *(Opposite above)* No. 46148 *The Manchester Regiment* is seen between the tunnels at Chester with a special from Holyhead on 27th July 1963; while *(below)* No. 46163 *Civil Service Rifleman* and No. 46120 *Royal Inniskilling Fusilier* put some 66,000 lb of tractive effort at the disposal of a Holyhead to Manchester express in June 1959.

Jim Carter

Plates 215 and 216: Over the bridge and through the town walls at Conway. *(Above)* The appropriately named No. 46138 *The London Irish Rifleman* emerges from the castellated portals of the tubular bridge with relief 'Irish Mail' in August 1964 while in the same month, *(below)* No. 46152 *The King's Dragoon Guardsman* approaches Conway station with a Manchester to Holyhead express.

Derek Cross

Plate 217 (above):   Holyhead based rebuild No. 46166 *London Rifle Brigade* awaits for the 'off' at Holyhead in 1948.

Eric Treacy

Plate 218 (below):   In later years the Holyhead depot, formerly 7C, became 6J at which time it played host to No. 46152 *The King's Dragoon Guardsman* seen here leaving Bangor with one of its diesel successors on the left.

Norman Kneale

Plate 219 (above): This famous LMS publicity picture, taken in November 1933, shows No. 6118 *Royal Welch Fusilier* leaving Robert Stephenson's famous Britannia tubular bridge over the Menai Straits. This celebrated structure is now much altered but its smaller brother at Conway still thankfully survives.

British Rail LMR

Plate 220 (below): No. 46127 *Old Contemptibles* has already been featured at Holyhead (see *Plates 188* and *189*). Here it is seen in 1948 making a vigorous start past the engine sheds with the up 'Irish Mail'.

Eric Treacy

OFF THE BEATEN TRACK

During their lifetime, the 'Royal Scots' were not wholly confined to their regular beats. Some of their wanderings were as a result of changed operating patterns on the railway system generally, others for more special circumstances. Not all of their migrations were recorded photographically, but quite a number of unusual events did manage to attract the photographers' attention, some of which are now recalled.

Plate 222 (below): On 30th September 1927, there was a Railwaymen's Exhibition at Belle Vue, Manchester. The LMS sent along the then new No. 6134 *Atlas* along with, of all things, a former LT&SR vacuum cleaner van!

Cowan Collection – National Railway Museum

Plate 221 (above): The writer cannot say why the LMS chose to line up No. 6135 *Samson*, LNWR No. 49 *Columbine* and a *Rocket* replica – but it makes an interesting picture, covering about 100 years of steam evolution. *Columbine* and a new *Rocket* replica (embodying parts of the one illustrated) are, happily, now at the National Railway Museum, York; but sadly (and wrongly in the author's view) officialdom in the early 1960s chose not to preserve a 'Royal Scot' in the National collection on the somewhat irrational grounds that none were left in the original condition – the mind boggles! *British Rail LMR*

The 1948 Locomotive Exchanges

Plates 223 to *228:* Of all the wanderings of the 'Royal Scots' none were more significant than those of rebuilds No. 46154 *The Hussar* and No. 46162 *Queen's Westminster Rifleman* in the 1948 locomotive exchanges. The LMS knew that in the rebuilt version of the 'Royal Scot' it had created a superb machine; but what no-one else had appreciated was that in rebuilt form, the 'Royal Scots' could compete on equal terms with nominally much more 'puissant' engines. The chosen representatives tackled on equal terms the sort of loads which put them on a similar footing with GWR 'Kings', LNER A4s and even Stanier's own 'Duchesses'. The late Cecil J. Allen, who was an ex-LNER man and who, therefore, could hardly be accused of prejudice, said of them:

'Relative to the moderate dimensions and weight and the simplicity of design of these 4-6-0s . . . I should be inclined to rate their best performance above anything else I witnessed during the test weeks . . .'

High praise indeed and for a 4-6-0 of no more than 83 tons to compete with and beat a GWR 'King' was a considerable achievement. Stanier with his Swindon background must have been very satisfied. All the more strange, therefore, that no-one saw fit officially to preserve one of these superb engines. Thankfully, private sponsors had no such inhibitions and we still have No. 6100 and No. 6115 for posterity to admire.

On these pages, these exchanges are illustrated. *(Left above)* No. 46162 arrives at King's Cross on 30th April 1948 while *(centre)* the engine is seen departing from the same station a week or so later. *(Below)* No. 46162 approaches Paddington on 20th May, interestingly passing a GWR 'Hall' Class in the design of which, William Stanier was much involved.

(Right above) No. 46162 leaves Paddington on the preliminary run on 19th May. In the centre and fitted with ex-WD tender because of lack of water troughs on the SR, No. 46154 leaves Waterloo with the down 'Atlantic Coast Express' on 7th June and *(below)* is seen at Exeter Central coupled to the ex-GWR dynamometer car on the up 'A.C.E'.

British Rail LMR, Photomatic and *P. L. Melvill*

Plates 229 and 230: In their final years, the 'Scots' were seen in all manner of places. (Above) No. 46141 *The North Staffordshire Regiment* took a train of Carlisle United supporters to Workington on the Maryport and Carlisle line on Boxing Day 1963. At the left is a reminder of the time when some of the 'Scots' were operating on the Great Central main line, prior to its unfortunate almost total closure. In this picture, No. 46156 *The South Wales Borderer* was observed near Loughborough on the 9.00 a.m. Sheffield to Bournemouth on 18th July 1964.

S. C. Crook and *Gerald Robinson*

Plates 231 and *232:* Special events involving 'Royal Scots' were quite common in their early years. *(Above)* No. 6159 *The Royal Air Force* seen at Derby is, for some reason, carrying the name *The Life Guardsman*, later given to the first Derby engine No. 6150. Amongst the identifiable dignitaries are, from the left: J. E. Anderson, H. G. Ivatt, two not identified by the author, Sir Henry Fowler, another unidentified gentleman and J. H. Follows. *(Below)* No. 6112 *Sherwood Forester* awaits the unveiling of the regimental crest at Derby c1934.

British Rail LMR

ON MIDLAND METALS – I

During their parallel boiler phase, the 'Royal Scots' were rarely used on the former Midland Railway main lines. It was not that the Midland line did not need newer motive power during the 1930s but more the fact that, as in pre-grouping years, the Midland line generally operated lighter trains. The 4-4-0 Compounds plus, later, the LMS Class 5XP 4-6-0s could cope more than adequately with the bulk of this type of traffic. Moreover, there were really no 'Royal Scots' to spare until the bulk of the Stanier 4-6-2s had been built — and this did not happen until well into the war.

Plates 233 to *235:* In fact, it was not until the twilight of steam that the 'Scots' regularly headed trains on the bulk of the old Midland system and this page shows some typical workings. *(Above)* No. 46132 *The King's Regiment Liverpool* leaves St. Pancras on 6th July 1960 with a down Manchester train while *(left above)* No. 46140 *The King's Royal Rifle Corps* passes Radlett a few weeks later with an up working over the same route.

British Rail LMR

(Below left): Leeds based No. 46109 *Royal Engineer* descends the Lickey Incline with a Leeds to Bristol express on 15th September 1962.

Gerald Robinson

Plate 236 (above): The first rebuild to emerge was No. 6103 *Royal Scots Fusilier* in June 1943. It went to Holbeck as one of an initial allocation of five engines and the men obviously liked it, for it never left Leeds for long! It is seen here as BR No. 46103 in the early 1950s on the down 'Thames-Clyde' express leaving Leeds City.

Eric Treacy

ON MIDLAND METALS – II

There was, however, one section of the Midland main line which needed something bigger than the 5XPs to cope with the heavy trains long before the late 1950s. I refer, of course, to the famous Leeds, Settle & Carlisle section. It was no coincidence that the very first of the rebuilds went, in 1943, to Leeds (Holbeck) to work the heavy wartime trains and it was on this route that I personally got to know them for the first time. It was their work over the Pennines that first alerted recorders to the fact that the LMS had something rather special in these engines, so the next section is by way of a tribute to the rebuilt engines and the route on which they first made their reputation.

Plates 237 to *240:* **Departures from Leeds.** Time can play tricks but if my memory serves aright, the first five genuine rebuilt 'Scots' to go to Leeds during 1943 were Nos. 6103, 6108, 6109, 6112 and 6117 (they also had *British Legion* for a few weeks but sent it back!). Later on, a few more were added and by the early 1950s, 'Scot' haulage was well nigh guaranteed on all the heavier trains. On these pages, four different members of the 'Leeds Club' are seen with the principal down daytime expresses.

(Opposite) No. 46130 *The West Yorkshire Regiment* (a later draftee to Leeds) departs with 'The Waverley' and No. 46133 *The Green Howards* (an early addition after the initial five) leaves with the 'Thames-Clyde'. On this page No. 46112 *Sherwood Forester* and No. 46109 *Royal Engineer* are seen with the 'Thames-Clyde' express leaving Leeds and passing Kirkstall Power Station, respectively.

Eric Treacy and *David Jenkinson*

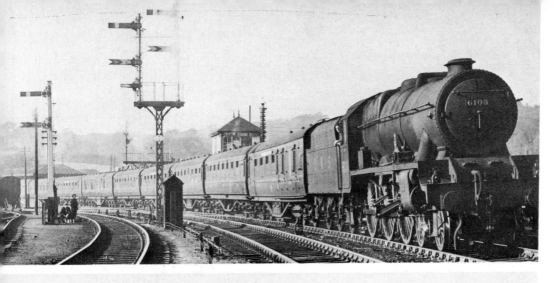

Plate 241: No. 6103 *Royal Scots Fusilier* rounds the curve at Skipton with the up 'Thames-Clyde' express c 1945/6.

Eric Treacy

Plates 242 and *243:* Sometimes the through trains were diverted between Skipton and Leeds via Bolton Abbey and Ilkley. Part of this route is, alas, no longer with us but these two views are a reminder of happier days. On this occasion, the diverted 'Thames-Clyde' seen at Addingham *(left)* and near Skipton *(below)* was in charge of another well-known Leeds 'Scot', No. 46117 *Welsh Guardsman*.

P. Sunderland

Plate 244: Hellifield — a bleak windy spot but a great place for train watching in former days. There was a midday local to Carlisle which started at Hellifield — and in the mid-1960s its motive power was highly unpredictable — anything from a Class 5 to a Brush Type 47 diesel. On this occasion c1962 it was distinguished by No. 46167 *The Hertfordshire Regiment.*
                              British Rail LMR

Plate 245: No. 6133 *The Green Howards,* immaculate in full LMS 1946 livery, departs from Hellifield with the down 'Thames-Clyde' express.

                              Eric Treacy

Plate 246: The up 'Waverley' express in the open rolling country-side between Gargrave and Bell Busk on 26th June 1961, with No. 46113 *Cameronian.*

                              Derek Cross

Plate 248 (above): No. 46113 *Cameronian* approaches the summit of the fourteen mile northbound climb past Blea Moor signal box with Ingleborough providing its unmistakable backdrop.

Alan Robey

Plate 247 (above): Footplate view from No. 6108 *Seaforth Highlander* on the climb from Settle to Blea Moor c 1946.

Eric Treacy

Plate 249 (below): The now preserved No. 46115 *Scots Guardsman* was nearing the end of its active life (and looking like it!) when photographed in August 1965 making heavy weather with a southbound freight on the last mile to Aisgill Summit.

Derek Cross

Plate 250 (above): No. 6103 *Royal Scots Fusilier* heads south past Armathwaite in late LMS days with the southbound 'Thames-Clyde' express.

E. E. Smith

Plate 251 (below): The same train is seen leaving Carlisle for the Midland route about two years later behind newly renumbered 46108 *Seaforth Highlander.*

Eric Treacy

Plate 252 (left): No. 6106 *Gordon Highlander* lays a smoke screen over the gantries at Crewe during the first year of its life.

Real Photographs

THE LIFE AND TIMES OF THE 'ROYAL SCOTS'

The 'Royal Scots' were born before the steam locomotive reached its zenith in Britain and in rebuilt form were one of the designs which were part of that zenith; and they survived to be one of the classes to disappear during the final holocaust of steam in the early 1960s. During their time the railways of Britain (like the country itself) underwent many changes and while one should not, perhaps, pursue the analogy too far, it does not seem too far fetched to say of the 'Royal Scots' that insofar as any one piece of railway equipment can be said to typify the whole, then these engines are as good a choice as any to stand for the last forty years of the British steam railway. We take our leave of them by following their progress from birth to death as it were — plus a mild form of resurrection too!

Plate 253 (left): No. 6111 *Royal Fusilier* with fourteen on at Castlethorpe c1934 typifies the time when virtually every train of note on the West Coast Main Line was 'Scot' powered.

Real Photographs

Plate 254 (below): Some fourteen years later, No. 6151 *The Royal Horse Guardsman* displays the final parallel boiler configuration at Newbold troughs in 1948.

Gordon Coltas

Plate 255 (above) This one has been published elsewhere before, but cropped too severely for my liking. I have taken the liberty of including much more of the negative in this majestic view of No. 6127 *Old Contemptibles* at Edge Hill c 1936.

Eric Treacy

Plates 256 to 258: In 1946 the LMS had a number of official pictures taken of various of its classes at work during this difficult time – not least the 'Scots'. *(Above)* No. 6111 *Royal Fusilier* is seen approaching Bushey with the 1.30 p.m. Euston to Liverpool on 23rd July 1946 while *(opposite above) Royal Scot* itself heads the sixteen coach 1.10 p.m. Euston to Blackpool at Bushey troughs on the same day. Two days later *(opposite below)* rebuild No. 6116 *Irish Guardsman* heads through Tring with the 8.20 a.m. Carlisle to Euston express.

British Rail LMR

Plate 259 (above): No. 6133 *The Green Howards* leaves Skipton with the down 'Thames-Clyde' express in 1946.

Eric Treacy

Plate 260 (left): The up version of the same train is seen some three to four years later at Kilmarnock behind No. 46117 *Welsh Guardsman*.

Eric Treacy

Plates 261 and *262:* Early 1950s scenes at Beattock: rebuilt No. 46166 *London Rifle Brigade (above)* and the last of the parallel boiler engines No. 46137 *The Prince of Wales Volunteers (right).*

Eric Treacy

Plates 263 to *267:* Scenes around London just before the diesels moved in in quantity. *(Opposite above)* No. 46146 *The Rifle Brigade* prepares to leave Euston while *(below)* No. 46163 *Civil Service Rifleman* seems to be having no problem with Camden Bank as it blows off vigorously on the climb out of Euston.

Eric Treacy

On this page, No. 6148 *The Manchester Regiment* passes Camden motive power depot in August 1955 *(top)* with a northbound express while No. 6101 *Royal Scots Grey* is seen at about the same time as it descends to Euston at journey's end.

R. C. Riley

The bottom picture, further out in the suburbs, illustrates No. 46159 *The Royal Air Force* heading south in 1956.

Photomatic

Plates *268* to *271*: This set of pictures shows more scenes from steam's St. Martin's summer in the 1950s. *(Above)* No. 46124 *London Scottish* leaves London Road, Manchester with a West of England train while *(left)* No. 46112 *Sherwood Forester* leaves Beattock station with a Carlisle to Glasgow stopping train — an odd job for a Leeds based engine, possibly commandeered at short notice. *(Opposite)* No. 46133 *The Green Howards* heads the appropriately embellished 'Thames-Clyde' through Bell Busk in Coronation week, 1953; while *(below)* *London Scottish* seen in October 1961 heading south from Shap to Oxenholme at Hay Fell with the up Perth to Euston is about to pass No. 46228 *Duchess of Rutland* on the down 'Mid-Day Scot'.

Eric Treacy and *Derek Cross*

Plates 272 to *274:* Like so many other types, the 'Royal Scots' found themselves doing more and more humdrum jobs as they approached the end of their careers and their ever more infrequent appearances at the head of express trains foretold their imminent demise. On this and the next few pages the declining years are featured.

The real rot set in during 1962 and the top view shows a typical working — No. 46121 *Highland Light Infantry* on a Carnforth to Glasgow fitted freight at Polquhap Summit in April 1962. The engine had less than eight months to survive.
Derek Cross

Another 1962 withdrawal was the pioneer rebuild No. 46103 *Royal Scots Fusilier* seen from two different views *(left)* on 20th July 1962 in charge of nothing more demanding than the so-called 'Harrison's Shunt' duty at Penrith — a far cry from taking the 'Thames-Clyde' over Aisgill.
Derek Cross

Plates 275 to 277: By 1964, massive withdrawals had taken place and the survivors were looking somewhat unkempt. *(Above)* No. 46118 *Royal Welch Fusilier* has no more than eight bogies on an up relief at Thrimby in March 1964 – but at least it's an express! *(Right)* No. 46162 *Queens Westminster ... an* is on freight duty at ...lquhap in April 1964 while *(below)* No. 46115 *Scots Guardsman* suffers the indignity of a pilot (2-6-4T No. 42449) in the Lune Gorge with the 9.30 a.m. Manchester to Glasgow on 9th August 1964.

John Whiteley and *Derek Cross*

Plates 278 to *282:* One of the last two survivors in traffic was No. 46140 *The King's Royal Rifle Corps* based at Carlisle. In 1965, photographers went 'Scot hunting' in the North West and *(left)* it is seen on 19th April 1965 (without nameplates) arriving at Carlisle with the morning Perth to Euston express. *Centre* and *below* the engine in June 1965 at Kingmoor Yard, departing with the Kingmoor to Maiden Lane perishable goods train. There is still some steam at Kingmoor shed *(bottom picture)* but Type 3 diesel No. D6790 symbolises the real situation.

G. Robinson and *Derek Cross*

No. 46140 lasted until November 1965 but even in July *(opposite above)* could be found nothing better than a permanent way special at Tebay. In due course it too found its way to the scrapyard like No. 46155 *The Lancer (below)* seen being towed to Troon for breaking up in company with rebuilt Patriot No. 45527 *Southport* in March 1965.

Derek Cross

. . . and there was only one left . . .

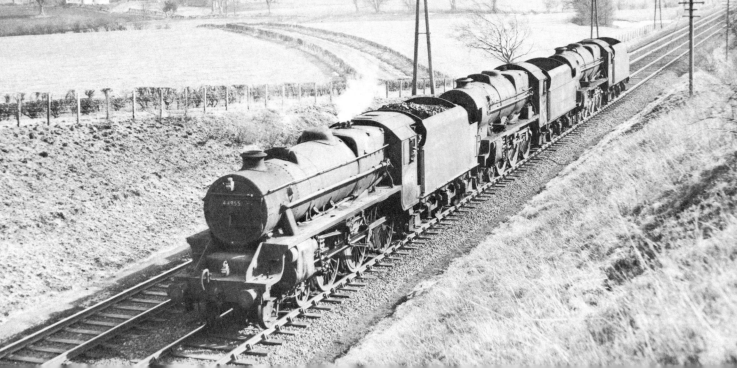

The One that got away

Scots Guardsman seemed likely to go the way of all the 'Royal Scots' (save for *Royal Scot* itself, now safely if somewhat inappropriately located at a Butlin holiday camp) but then private enterprise stepped in again in the form of the late Mr. Bill.

In its final years in traffic *(Plates 283, 284 left)* No. 46115 was at Carlisle doing the same humdrum duties as the other survivors like the 'Horse & Carriage' train at Carlisle No. 13 box *(upper)* or a Warrington bound freight *(lower)*, both in 1964-5.

S. C. Crook

When withdrawn, the engine was stabled on the Worth Valley Railway for a while and then went to the Dinting railway centre from whence, in due course, after a lengthy but magnificent restoration, 1978 saw a return to the main line *(this page)*. To the right, *(Plates 285* and *286)*, two views taken on 28th September at Chinley show the trial trip. Interestingly, the BR Sulzer diesels *(upper view)* took the names of some of the scrapped 'Royal Scots'.

Larry Goddard

Finally, and with tender now fully painted, the engine was given its first main line outings and was seen *(below, Plate 287)* on 11th November approaching Cowburn Tunnel with the Guide Bridge to York 'Yorkshire Venturer'.

David Eatwell

Plates 288 and 289: The author can claim some modest responsibility for having suggested, back in the 1960s, that No. 6115 should be given, uniquely in the world of preservation, the fully lined 1946 LMS express livery *(see Plate 79)*. It has been magnificently applied by the dedicated volunteers at Dinting and the restored engine now presents a noble sight as witnessed by these two fine views at Dinting by night on 20th April 1981. Long may it so remain.

Jim Carter

ROYAL SCOT CLASS 4-6-0 – GENERAL SUMMARY OF ENGINES

LMS No.	Name	Original Name (until 1935/6)	Date Rebuilt	Date Re-No.	Scrap	
6100†	Royal Scot		6/50	16/48	10/62	(i)
6101	Royal Scots Grey		11/45	5/48	9/63	
6102†	Black Watch		10/49	9/48	12/62	
6103	Royal Scots Fusilier		6/43	10/48	12/62	(ii)
6104	Scottish Borderer		3/46	8/48	12/62	
6105†	Cameron Highlander		3/48	5/48	12/62	
6106†	Gordon Highlander		9/49	6/48	12/62	
6107†	Argyll and Sutherland Highlander		2/50	4/48	12/62	
6108	Seaforth Highlander		8/43	5/48	1/63	
6109	Royal Engineer		7/43	5/48	12/62	
6110†	Grenadier Guardsman		1/53	3/49	2/64	
6111	Royal Fusilier		10/47	11/48	10/63	
6112	Sherwood Forester		9/43	9/48	5/64	
6113†	Cameronian		12/50	5/49	12/62	
6114	Coldstream Guardsman		6/46	6/48	10/63	
6115	Scots Guardsman		8/47	1/49	1/66	(iii)
6116	Irish Guardsman		8/44	9/48	9/63	
6117	Welsh Guardsman		12/43	5/48	11/62	
6118	Royal Welch Fusilier		12/46	2/49	6/64	
6119	Lancashire Fusilier		9/44	7/48	12/63	
6120	Royal Inniskilling Fusilier		11/44	6/48	7/63	
6121	Highland Light Infantry, The City of Glasgow Regiment	(H.L.I. in LMS period)	8/46	10/48	12/62	
6122	Royal Ulster Rifleman		9/45	4/48	11/64	
6123†	Royal Irish Fusilier		5/49	6/48	10/62	
6124	London Scottish		12/43	4/48	12/62	
6125	3rd Carabinier	Lancashire Witch	8/43	9/48	10/64	
6126	Royal Army Service Corps	Sanspareil	6/45	11/48	10/63	
6127	Old Contemptibles	Novelty	8/44	5/48	12/62	
6128	The Lovat Scouts	Meteor	6/46	2/49	5/65	
6129	The Scottish Horse	Comet	12/44	6/48	6/64	
6130†	The West Yorkshire Regiment	Liverpool	12/49	5/48	12/62	
6131	The Royal Warwickshire Regiment	Planet	10/44	8/48	10/62	
6132	The King's Regiment Liverpool	Phoenix	11/43	4/48	2/64	
6133	The Green Howards	Vulcan	7/44	1/49	2/63	
6134†	The Cheshire Regiment	Atlas	12/54	11/48	11/62	
6135	The East Lancashire Regiment	Samson	1/47	9/48	12/62	
6136†	The Border Regiment	Goliath	3/50	7/48	4/64	
6137†	The Prince of Wales's Volunteers South Lancashire	Vesta	3/55	5/48	10/62	(iv)
6138	The London Irish Rifleman	Fury (until 1929)	6/44	1/49	2/63	
6139	The Welch Regiment	Ajax	11/46	5/48	10/62	
6140†	The King's Royal Rifle Corps	Hector	5/52	1/49	11/65	
6141†	The North Staffordshire Regiment	Caledonian	10/50	7/48	4/64	
6142†	The York & Lancaster Regiment	Lion	2/51	7/48	1/64	
6143†	The South Staffordshire Regiment	Mail	6/49	9/48	12/63	
6144	Honourable Artillery Company	Ostrich	6/45	6/48	1/64	
6145	The Duke of Wellington's Regt. (West Riding)	Condor	1/44	9/49	11/62	
6146	The Rifle Brigade	Jenny Lind	10/43	6/48	11/62	
6147	The Northamptonshire Regiment	Courier	9/46	1/49	11/62	
6148†	The Manchester Regiment	Velocipede	7/54	6/48	12/64	
6149	The Middlesex Regiment	Lady of the Lake	4/45	4/48	9/63	
6150	The Life Guardsman		12/45	1/49	12/62	
6151†	The Royal Horse Guardsman		4/53	10/48	12/62	
6152	The King's Dragoon Guardsman		8/45	6/48	4/65	(v)
6153†	The Royal Dragoon		8/49	6/48	12/62	
6154†	The Hussar		3/48	4/48	11/62	(vi)
6155†	The Lancer		8/50	7/48	12/64	

6156†	The South Wales Borderer		5/54	1/49	10/64
6157	The Royal Artilleryman		1/46	12/48	1/64
6158†	The Loyal Regiment		9/52	10/48	11/63
6159	The Royal Air Force		10/45	9/48	5/65
6160	Queen Victoria's Rifleman		2/45	9/48	5/65
6161	King's Own		10/46	7/48	11/62
6162†	Queen's Westminster Rifleman		1/48	4/48	6/64
6163†	Civil Service Rifleman		10/53	11/48	9/64
6164†	The Artist's Rifleman		6/51	4/48	12/62
6165†	The Ranger (12th London Regt.)		6/52	10/48	12/64
6166	London Rifle Brigade		1/45	7/48	10/64
6167†	The Hertfordshire Regiment		12/48	12/48	4/64
6168	The Girl Guide		4/46	9/48	5/64
6169	The Boy Scout		5/45	5/48	7/63
6170	British Legion	Fury (as 6399) 1935	4/48	11/62	(vii)

Notes

† Still with parallel boiler at close of LMS period

(i) Original 6152 until 1933. Preserved as LMS 6100 by Sir Billy Butlin but still in rebuilt condition
The first of the class to be withdrawn and now located at Bressingham

(iii) Last engine to be withdrawn (actually on 1/1/66) and preserved, first to get smoke deflectors
in rebuilt state (8/47). Now located at Dinting Railway Centre

(iv) Last engine to be rebuilt

(v) Original 6100 until 1933

(vi) Actually withdrawn for rebuilding in 1947

(vii) Prototype rebuilt engine

Building dates: 6101-49/6152 built 1927 by NB Locomotive Co.
6100/6150-1/6153-69 built 1930 at Derby Works
6170 and all other rebuilds were completed at Crewe Works